CRUISING AROUND SOUTH AFRICA
2019-20
Including Cruising the Coast of Namibia

Contents

Introduction	3
Preparing to Cruise	7
Africa in Quick Review	13
The Republic of South Africa	26
Historic Sketch of South Africa	39
Touring Around Cape Town	45
Around Cape Town	70
What to See Around Mossel Bay	92
A Visit to Port Elizabeth	100
A Brief Stop in East London	115

Touring Around Durban	125
Visiting Remote Richards Bay	150
Traveling Through Greater Johannesburg	161
The National Capital Pretoria	196
Namibia as a Nation	212
A Visit to Walvis Bay	220
Stopping in Remote Lüderitz	234
Final Words	244
About the Author	245

The majority of photographs were taken by the author on various trips to South Africa

All Wikimedia.com photographs used in this book contain the name of the author or copyright holder and are herein used in accordance with Creative Commons Attribution Share Alike license 2.0, 3.0 or 4.0.

OpenStreetMap contributor maps are used and so identified in accordance with the copyright use authorization. www.openstreetmap.org maps can be downloaded to your smart phone, ipad or laptop and used while traveling. You have the capability of zooming in to enhance detail. They are useful while out sightseeing and are so much easier to use than carrying paper maps.

INTRODUCTION

Cruising around South Africa is for many travelers the ultimate journey simply because of the great distance from either Europe or North America where the vast majority of those who regularly cruise live. At first glance it seems like a daunting journey, especially when one views the long flights to South Africa and returning home. There are of course longer cruises that begin and/or end in Europe. Unless you are retired, it is not that convenient to spend between 45 and 80 days onboard a ship to either circumnavigate the African continent or to travel one way between a European port and South Africa. The last time I made such a journey, I left Civitavecchia, Italy in mid-November and left the ship in Cape Town in early January after having first cruised from Cape Town to Richards Bay and back twice along with a second detour cruise to Namibia. But as a retired geography professor and lecturer for a five-star cruise line, I had plenty of time to accomplish such a visit.

Only a few major cruise lines, primarily high-end companies, include southern Africa in their annual itineraries. Silversea, Seaborne, Regent Seven Seas and Holland America have such cruise offerings for 2019 and 2020. The best time of the year to book such a cruise is between mid-November and the end of March. Remember that in the Southern Hemisphere this time of year is summer, and it is a good time of year to travel around South Africa. Most people initially think of Africa in a tropical context, but the maps will clearly reveal that the Republic of South Africa is a subtropical country, most of its territory being in temperate latitudes. You could compare the climate of the west coast to that of California and to its east coast to that of South Carolina or Florida in the United States, but without hurricanes. And the Cape Town region on the west coast is not plagued by the danger of earthquakes as is California. The interior of South Africa contains semi-arid grassland much like the south central Great Plains of the United States. Between the grasslands and the western coast and extending into Namibia there are vast deserts, which are very similar to those of the American Southwest.

Many cruises around South Africa will often include one or two ports in neighboring Namibia on the Atlantic side of the continent. Namibia is an arid country, north of the Tropic of Capricorn. It is very sparsely populated, but yet has a modern infrastructure very similar to that of South Africa. Both of Namibia's ports of call are also included in this book following the material on South Africa.

This book is designed for those visitors who are planning or considering a cruise to South Africa. It will provide you with information regarding the major ports of call from the Atlantic around to the Indian Ocean side of the country. And since the majority of visitors then remain and travel into the interior, normally to visit a game park, there are chapters on the cities of Johannesburg and Pretoria as well as information on the major interior game parks.

I trust that this book will be beneficial in helping you to become acquainted with the landscapes, history and cultures of the two countries to be visited. And you come to gain an understanding of the rich history and diversity of the cultures that make the region so fascinating

This is not a typical guidebook such as Fyodor or Frommer's. You will find restaurant recommendations for the ports of call, but only those that offer top quality and atmosphere. Their hotel recommendations are provided only for Cape Town and Johannesburg, as many cruise itineraries begin or end in Cape Town and then most overseas flights are routed from Johannesburg, which is the nation's largest city and major air gateway.

The chapters on each port of call offer geographic and historic background combined with concise descriptions of the ports of call, showing you their major highlights and recommending various modes of transport to enable you to get the most out of the day's sightseeing. The vast majority of experienced cruisers do not especially enjoy the group tours provided by the cruise lines and prefer to be more independent. But in South Africa it is necessary to use great caution in how you proceed on your own because of the unfortunate crime situation. I provide very helpful and honest recommendations as to how to tour independently while remaining safe. South Africa is an amazingly beautiful country with vibrant cultures that enrich your experience. But at the same time if you go off without being aware of its darker side, you can end up in great trouble.

The primary focus of this book is to offer you an overall introduction to the lands and peoples you will be seeing. And all my recommendations regarding independent sightseeing, dining while ashore and hotels at the start and conclusion of your cruise are all based upon personal experience. I only recommend what I believe to be the very best establishments. This book will give you a very good working knowledge of the historic and cultural details of each place to be visited. Essentially you will be a well-informed visitor before you even reach the shores of South Africa and Namibia.

Lew Deitch
Revised February 2019

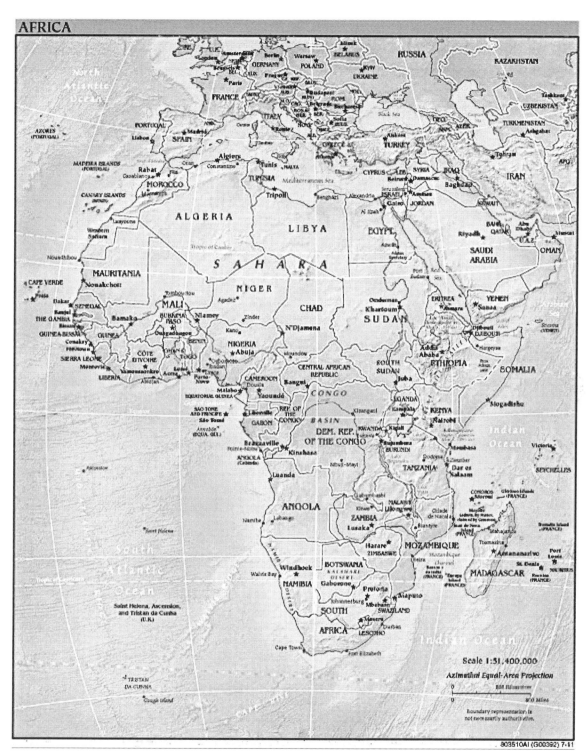

A General Physical Political Map of Africa

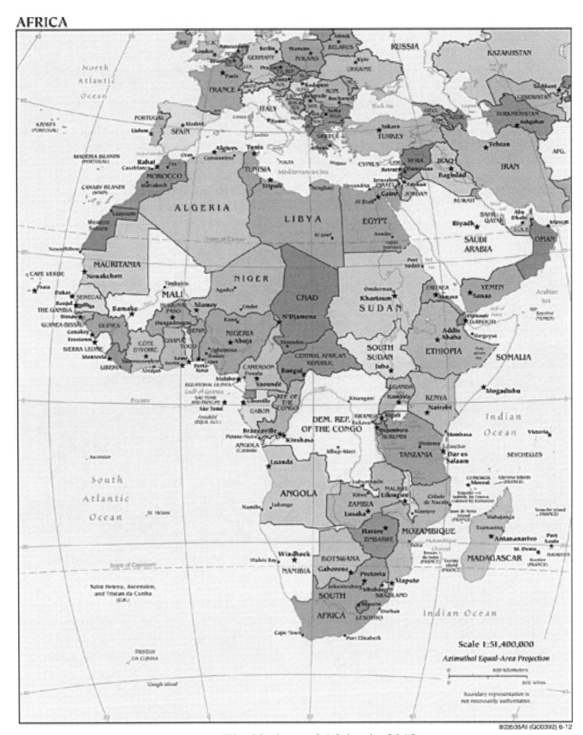

The Nations of Africa in 2019

PREPARING TO CRUISE

For those of us living in North America or Europe, there is a certain mystique about Africa. Not long ago it was referred to as "The Dark Continent," reflecting the lack of knowledge of the planet's second largest continental land mass. Even now there are many misconceptions regarding the nature of the landscape and its diverse cultures. To set the stage for this tour book, the next chapter will present a brief review of the basic geographic and historic factors that combine to make Africa a very distinctive continent, one that should be better understood by the rest of the world.

This book has been prepared for those who are planning a cruise where the major portion of the itinerary will be centered upon the ports of the Republic of South Africa and Namibia. As previously noted, it is designed to provide you with geographic and historic information so that you become better informed about the major places you will be visiting.

PREPARING TO CRUISE: What do you need to do to prepare for your cruise? This question involves numerous sub topics that will be explained. There are many questions people have regarding visas, the flights, what to pack with regard to weather conditions, currency issues and health concerns. I will address those issues here. If you have specific and personalized questions, please contact me at my web page. I will respond with answers to your personal questions. The web site is http://www.doctorlew.com.

VISAS: For citizens holding United States, Canadian or European Union passports, you will require a visa for both South Africa and Namibia. However, the visas are issued upon arrival when you clear immigration in the first port of call of each country, or if you initially arrive in South Africa by air. For those holding other passports, you need to check with national government or your cruise line for more specific details.

FLIGHTS TO AND FROM THE SHIP: The South African circumnavigation cruises all start and conclude in Cape Town. One-way journeys begin in either Civitavecchia (Rome) for west coast itineraries or in Piraeus (Athens) traveling southbound along Africa's eastern coast. If you are coming northbound along either the west or east coast of Africa, your journey will begin in Cape Town. If you will be boarding and/or disembarking from the ship in Cape Town, there are direct flights from London and Frankfurt operating on an overnight basis. The flight takes around 12 hours, and is surprisingly smooth most of the time, as you are flying over the great bulk of the African landmass with the exception of crossing the narrow part of the Mediterranean Sea. Lufthansa, British Airways and South African Airways all offer non-stop flights into Cape Town. If you are planning to do a land tour or visit a game park in the interior prior to joining the ship or following your cruise, you will be flying between Europe or North America and Johannesburg, which is the country's largest international airport. The length of non-stop flights from New York to Johannesburg is around 18 hours. There are also non-stop flights between Sydney, Australia and Johannesburg. I highly recommend Business Class because most airlines today offer the full flat beds, which are so much more comfortable than being in coach or even in the upgraded coach class. Yes it is more expensive, but there are non-refundable Business Class fares if you purchase well ahead of traveling.

WEATHER: As noted before, South Africa is a subtropical country, its latitudes similar to those of the southern portion of the United States. The west coast has a Mediterranean climate, which means warm days and comfortable nights, a range from the mid 30's to mid-teens Celsius or 80's to mid 50's Fahrenheit between day and night with little rain. The east coast has a decidedly more humid climate, but once again temperatures are normally in the mid 20's Celsius or 75 to 80 degree Fahrenheit range. And periodic rain showers are more likely. In the northern interior it does get hot during the day with temperatures in the upper 20's to mid 30's Celsius or 80's and 90's Fahrenheit, but it does cool down at night because of the altitudes being 1,500 to 2,000 meter or 3,000 to 6,000 feet above sea level.

WHAT TO PACK: You will be well advised to pack light clothes, preferably cotton in pastel colors, as they breathe easier and help keep you cool. If you are prone to any adverse reaction to heat or sunlight, a comfortable hat is recommended. And it is also wise to have a good sunscreen. And in the interior it does get surprisingly cool at night and a light sweater or long sleeve shirt is recommended. These cruises occur during the Southern Hemisphere summer, but South Africa is surprisingly comfortable except in the Kalahari Desert region. Namibia can be quite a bit warmer in the near coastal Namib Desert and its portion of the Kalahari Desert

Depending upon your cruise line, you may need formal or smart casual dress for evening events on board. This of course varies with each cruise operator. And attending such evening events is always optional. In the major cities people dress quite casual, but there are very fine restaurants in Cape Town, Durban and Johannesburg where smart casual or even dressy attire is expected.

On deck, a light sweater or windbreaker is advisable, especially once the ship sails into temperate latitudes. The South African coast can be relatively cool in the evenings during the summer months. And off the coast of Namibia it can sometimes be a bit chilly, as the breeze blows over cold ocean currents and fog is not uncommon.

FOOD AND WATER: In South Africa you will find that urban sanitation standards are comparable to those of North America and northern Europe. You can feel totally safe in ordering salads and fruits, as they will have been washed in water that meets our standards of safety. In rural areas the same holds true in restaurants that you would find in small cities and towns. If you plan to eat while visiting any tribal reserves where running water is not available, it would be advisable to eat only cooked foods. Bottled water is available everywhere not because of need, but like in North America and Europe it is simply preferred. Only in remote tribal areas is the water not safe to drink.

HEALTH CONCERNS: There are no major health concerns that should impact you as a visitor. It is recommended, however, that if you visit game reserves along the northeastern coast near the Mozambique border there is a risk of malaria from mosquito bites. Insect repellant is highly advised. Some people go to the extreme of taking the anti-malarial tablets before and during a visit to these areas. If you have any specific concerns, ask your doctor before leaving home or the doctor on board the ship. The anti-malarial medication does have numerous potentially uncomfortable side effects. Although you hear a lot in the news about aids being quite common in South Africa, it will not impact your visit unless you were to engage in unsavory activities. Need I say more?

Always take out a traveler's health insurance policy before departure from home. And make certain that your policy has a sizable allowance for medical evacuation. This is just a normal precaution when traveling so far from home. Hospitals in South Africa meet exceptionally high standards with regard to their services and the levels of sanitation. Remember that the first heart transplant ever performed was by famous surgeon Christian Barnhart in Cape Town.

CURRENCY: The official currency of the Republic of South Africa is the Rand. You will need it for any local purchases, taxi fare or when using public transport. Foreign currency is not accepted. All major restaurants and stores do accept international credit cards. When utilizing an ATM for currency, you will receive Rand in all cases. In Namibia the official currency is the Namibian Dollar, which is pegged to the South African Rand in exchange rates. My recommendation is to order small amounts of local currency from your bank at home prior to departure.

POSTAGE: If you wish to send post cards or letters you are best doing it on board the ship. The South African and Namibian postal services are quite reliable. But you need to specify airmail otherwise it will take weeks for a post card to arrive home.

CRIME: We hear or read about the high crime rates in South Africa. Since the end of white rule and the strict Apartheid regulations the people of South Africa have greater personal freedom and mobility. However, the economic picture has been slow to change and many still live in abject poverty. This has created a situation where high crime statistics reflect the economic inequities. Violent crimes against visitors are not generally a problem, but there are neighborhoods or townships in all of South Africa where a visitor regardless of your race is subject to being robbed at gunpoint or knifepoint and resistance can lead to serious injury or death.

As in any country where you are a stranger, certain precautions are necessary to avoid becoming a victim of crime. In South Africa it is essential to be more vigilant than you would be in any European country. Here are some rules to be observed that will make your journey safe and successful:

* When out in public, do not wear expensive jewelry or watches.

* Do not flash large amounts of money when making a purchase.

* Keep money, passport or other valuable documents well hidden, using an inside pouch or money belt.

* Do not carry large handbags.

* Keep cameras close, preferably worn around your neck.

* When visiting townships or tribal reserves it is best to be in the company of a licensed guide, most of which are of Black African origin. They speak the local languages and know all of the potential danger signs. Hiring drivers or guides is relatively inexpensive by our standards, and not only will they enrich your experience, but they will look out for your safety. Last time I was in Johannesburg for eight days I hired a driver/guide from the Zulu Nation. He took me into parts of the city where no foreigner, especially one who is white, would dare to venture on their own. It was an incredibly enriching experience and at no time did I ever feel ill at ease. We even rode in the "combies," locally run transport vans for the poorer Black African people. And I was shown nothing but hospitality.

* When in the busy central downtown areas of major cities the above recommendations are essential, as these tend to be higher crime areas. Take the necessary precautions, but DO NOT be so fearful that you avoid the experience. It will bring you so much closer to understanding some of socio-economic problems that face South Africa since the end of the rigid Apartheid system.

8 If you go out at night make certain it is safe to do so by checking with your hotel front desk. The more upscale districts of the major cities are safe for walking at night, but you need to know where these areas are located.

* If using public trains, pay the extra fee to ride in first class carriages. Your safety should always be paramount. If you have a guide with you and wish to experience the local transportation without using first class, it is safe to do so while in their company.
These recommendations may sound a bit intimidating, but they are good precautions to follow. People in South Africa are friendly and helpful to visitors. But there are those seeking to profit by mugging or picking pockets, even violent means. Thus it is advisable to be vigilant, yet not become paranoid. If you are touring in the company of a licensed guide, you can feel more relaxed, as would be criminals will avoid coming in contact with you when they see that a local person who is Black African accompanies you.

RACIAL RELATIONS: The vast majority of the guides are members of the various native tribes, especially Xhosa and Zulu. And you will learn so much about the country when in their company. It is also much easier to visit a township or tribal homeland in their company. In Cape Town and Johannesburg many guides are Afrikaans, people of Dutch origin. And you will often see a different side to the South African way of life when in their company. From my experience, I have found that since the end of Apartheid there is a strong sense of national unity. People have come together and they do respect one another across racial and ethnic lines. Thanks to the teachings of the late Nelson Mandela, there is a greater sense of brotherhood among the majority of South Africans. But there are still those on both sides of the racial divide who still harbor animosity to those of the white race based upon all of the indignities of the past when Blacks and Coloured were treated with great disrespect. Mandela put forth a wonderful concept when he said that the Black majority should not forget the indignities of the past years of Apartheid, but that they must forgive. And you will see evidence of this everywhere. South African whites are now not the political majority, but they have come to a peaceful acceptance of the equality of the races, having had the highest respect for Mr. Mandela. I have found that there is a greater sense of unity and oneness than there is in the United States, despite the minority on both sides that still harbor resentments.

The South African Rand

The Namibian Dollar

AFRICA IN QUICK REVIEW

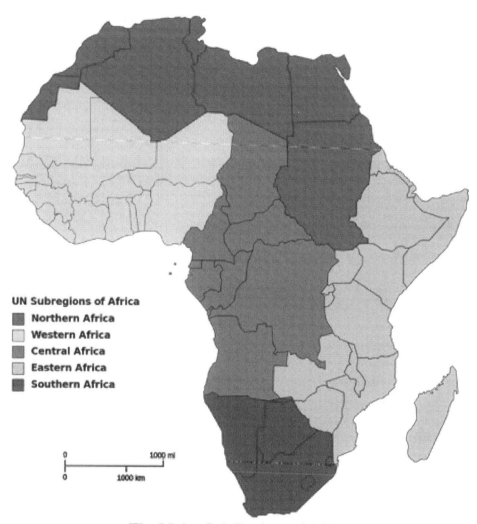

The Major Sub Regions of Africa

THE LANDSCAPE: Africa is the second largest landmass on earth, covering 30,221,532 square kilometers or 11,668,599 square miles. It has an estimated population today in excess of 1,100,000 people. There are many distinct geographic and cultural regions of the continent, making this a continent of great diversity. The regions shown on the map at the start of this chapter represent a combination of environmental and cultural factors, but the boundaries follow those of nations, which is somewhat artificial. Natural regions do not stop at national frontiers, nor do cultural differences. But the use of national boundaries to create these major sub regions is justifiable with qualification. These sub regions recognized by the United Nations, are:

* Northern Africa: This sub region includes the Mediterranean coast and extends both into the Sahara Desert and well into the middle reaches of the River Nile. This is a region in which desert and tropical savanna landscapes predominate, inhabited primarily by Berber and Arab people. On the southern margins, Islam has spread through the Sahara Desert among the northern Black races of Africa.

* Western Africa: Here is a region that begins deep in the Sahara Desert and extends into the western tropics of the continent. The numerous Black tribal groups on the northern margins have accepted Islam whereas along the humid tropical coast Christianity has blended with native animistic traditions. There has always been trade between the desert and humid land dwellers, and this is also where the slave trade reached its absolute peak. It is vital to recognize that slavery is a universal ill, and in Western Africa, it was many of the coastal Black kingdoms that profited by raiding lesser tribes and capturing their people to then sell to white European slave traders.

* Central Africa: Again the region begins deep in the Sahara Desert and extends through the humid tropical reaches of the Congo Basin and toward the southern savanna. The Black tribal groups have had less interaction, but this region is better defined by its former strong French, Belgian and Portuguese colonial heritage.

* Eastern Africa: This region represents the upland plateaus and the Great Rift Valley, extending from the arid north into the tropics of the equatorial latitudes and south into the savanna. But elevation has played a major role in shaping the cultures, as here is where the domestication of cattle brought about strong societies whose cultures were based upon a herding tradition. And the predominant colonial influences were British and German. The far southern part of the mainland was under Portuguese colonial rule. On the island of Madagascar, a distinct highland tradition also existed, but it was under French colonial influences.

* Southern Africa: Strong British and Dutch colonial influences molded the traditional herding societies, as it was here where a large and dominant white European population claimed superiority for over two centuries of rule. Today this area is considered to be the most modern and economically secure on the continent with the exception of Zimbabwe where dictatorial rule has precluded great strides in social or economic development.

These subdivisions of the continent are far from perfect. But other attempts at defining the regions of the continent are equally flawed. The complexity of the physical geography and the assemblages of cultures makes it difficult to divide Africa into very meaningful regions. With regard to the physical landscapes of the continent, Africa is very distinct in that it contains the world's largest desert, the second largest tropical rainforest, the Great Rift Valley with some of the world's largest lakes and the greatest variety of natural wildlife.

North Africa is predominantly desert with the exception of a small band of mild, Mediterranean climate that stretches from the coast of Morocco across Algeria into Tunisia. This is the result of the Atlas Mountains, Africa's only major block of mountains, sheltering the coastal margins from the drying winds that blow across the Sahara Desert.

The great deserts of the Sahara are not all sandy, as is often pictured in Hollywood movies. There are rugged rocky outcrops and gravel plains interspersed with the seas of sand. And dotting the landscape are the oases where underground water bubbles to the surface and supports life. The River Nile rises in the highlands of eastern Africa and flows as a ribbon of life giving water across over 6,400 kilometers or 4,000 miles of the eastern Sahara. It was here that the great Egyptian civilization arose over 6,000 years ago.

The Sahara slowly gives way to a tropical grassland or savanna on its southern margin. This vast region stretches from Senegal on the Atlantic coast to the highlands of Ethiopia. Overgrazing for thousands of years has weakened the natural landscape and it is subject to periodic droughts, creating massive problems of famine and disease. Global climate change combined with increased population pressures is causing the region to become even more unstable with droughts creating massive famines. And of course political instability and religious tensions are creating major problems in such countries as Mali, Chad and South Sudan. Militant Islamic groups have terrorized many tribal areas, even as far south as northern Nigeria.

The western bulge of the continent experiences a humid tropical climate with a strong high sun or summer monsoonal influence. It is here in the highlands that the Niger River rises, but it flows north toward the Sahara Desert before turning around and flowing back into the humid tropics of Nigeria. This is a region in which there is a mix of savanna in the north, tropical scrub in the middle reaches and then tropical rainforest along the coast.

The eastern highlands that stretch from Ethiopia southward into Mozambique present a landscape that is a mix of desert along the Red Sea and Indian Ocean coastlines, but slowly gives way to true tropical rainforest in the equatorial zone. In the high plateaus the land grades from desert to upland savanna and woodland where life for both animals and humans has been good. But this is also the zone where the great African Rift Valley exists, created by the earth's crust pulling itself slowly apart. There are numerous volcanic fields and several individual high volcanic peaks, the highest being Mt. Kilimanjaro, which is the highest point in Africa with an elevation of 5,895 meters or 19,341. It is classed along with the other high peaks as being dormant, but not extinct. In many of the deep parts of the rift, water has accumulated to form massive lakes, which are among the world's largest, such as Victoria, Tanganyika and Malawi along with many lesser bodies of water.

The center of the continent contains a large river basin that lies within the equatorial belt, one of the great rivers of the planet. The Congo Basin is second only to the Amazon Basin as a vast tropical rainforest. And the Congo River is second only to the Amazon in the volume of water it drains to the ocean.

South of the Congo Basin, the land again rises in elevation onto a plateau with a wet/dry woodland and savanna climate. Farther to the south on the western side of the continent the landscape changes to desert, but not as barren and hostile as the Sahara. The great Kalahari Desert is more like parts of the American Southwest in that it is borderline semi-arid and contains a mix of grassland and scattered woodland. Only along the immediate coast is there true desert, nearly as barren as the Sahara. Here the cold Benguela Current creates the Namib Desert, which receives very scant rainfall. It is akin to the Atacama Desert of Peru and northern Chile, being the second of the world's driest lands.

To the east, the savanna landscape continues south in the highlands, slowly becoming less tropical and more temperate, as it extends south of the Tropic of Capricorn. Eventually it grades into pure grassland known in South Africa as the Veld. And the Kalahari Desert also ultimately merges with the high altitude Veld. There is one great river that flows from the tropical interior, draining to the east. This river is vital to the lives of the people in Zambia, Zimbabwe and South Africa. It is the Zambezi, plunging over the dramatic Victoria Falls, the world's greatest cataract.

Along the southwestern coast of South Africa, the plateau that is the Veld merges to the southwest with the semi-arid Great Karoo. Once over the Great Escarpment the climate becomes a mild, wet winter and dry summer Mediterranean type. But along the Indian Ocean coastline to the east, the landscape turns more humid and is similar to the subtropical climates of the southeastern United States. It is here that Africa's second major mountain range, the Drakensberg, is found. Unlike other continents, Africa is composed primarily of plateaus and only has two significant ranges of mountains. The two major rivers flowing off the Veld are the Orange, which flows to the Atlantic and the Limpopo, which flows to the Indian Ocean.

CULTURAL DIVERSITY: The human landscape of Africa is far more complicated than the natural landscape. Many of us in the North American or European world think of Africa as somewhat homogenous with Arab peoples in the north and the Black tribes south of the Sahara. But in reality there is a great variety in what are still called racial characteristics along with those that are cultural. Anthropologists question the very notion of race, as we are of course on human species. There are many variations in hair texture, eye color, facial features and skin color that led our ancestors to create the notion of human races. But drawing the distinction between races is increasingly more difficult with inter racial marriages so much more commonplace than 100 years ago.

Simply stated for Africa, the people living north of the Sahara have lighter skin and facial features related to the people of the Middle East. And culturally many are transplanted

Arabs while others are native Berber who have culturally blended many of their lifestyle traits with the Arabs.

South of the Sahara Desert, the various people of Africa all have dark skin, very curly hair and a variety of physical features that have traditionally been associated with the so called Negro race. There is tremendous variation in height, body mass and facial features, creating distinctive physical groupings.

Culturally Sub Saharan Africa contains hundreds of individual languages and cultures. The diversity is greater than that of Europe, yet people of European heritage tend to see all of Sub Saharan Africa as rather homogenous. Prior to the coming of the Europeans, there were great kingdoms that dominated in western and southern Africa. Names such as the Ashanti of Ghana or the Zulu of South Africa represent actual nations that were built upon a hereditary system not unlike many nations in Europe. Today most have been absorbed into nations that grew out of the borders set by the European colonial territories. But in the far south, the nations of Lesotho and Swazi do represent individual kingdoms. In eastern Africa there were very strong tribes whose lifestyle was based upon herding. Although not true nations, they did maintain an individual identity and held tenaciously to their territory. The Maasai of Kenya and Tanzania are one of the best known such tribes.

The map of modern Africa is primarily the result of European intervention during the 19th century. The British, French, Belgian, German and Portuguese powers each claimed vast tracts of African land, creating colonial empires. In most cases there were infusions of Europeans who settled, built the economy and dominated the native peoples. It was only after World War II that the European powers began to divest themselves of their colonies, giving independence to the local people. But the boundaries often crossed tribal or old kingdom borders, and now people were expected to show loyalty to totally artificial governments. And in many cases, the native people were unprepared for nationhood. The end result has been over six decades of ethnic warfare, political unrest and corruption. Only a handful of countries have been successful in handling independence.

Of all the countries on the continent, South Africa developed the strongest infrastructure and economy. And this is the result of British and Dutch colonists coming in great numbers and developing a powerful economy that was fueled by near slave labor under the Apartheid system. With the fall of Apartheid and the establishment of Black rule, the people of all ethnic groups have worked together, but with some difficulties, to continue building upon the infrastructure that was already in place. Rather than force the Europeans out, there has been a merging of peoples and it has proven successful, as much of this book will establish. But in South Africa there are those among the Black African leadership that still fuel the tensions by wanting to divest the white community of many of its economic powers and ownership of land. They only need to look to the north at neighboring Zimbabwe where the former dictator Robert Mugabe ruined the country by stripping the whites of their wealth and land. The country today can best be described as being one step above anarchy. And if such a policy as he introduced into Zimbabwe should ever evolve in South Africa it would destroy the total economic fabric. Right now South Africa has the strongest and most viable economy of any nation in Africa.

Despite the many problems facing most of Africa, the potential for greatness is there. The continent is blessed with many natural resources and is able to provide sufficient food to feed its massive population. It is simply a matter of developing a better educational base, cleaning up corruption and encouraging capital investment to enable Africa to compete in global markets. And in countries such as South Africa, Namibia and Kenya the white population must be an integral part of any future development if these countries are to continue to grow.

The eastern margins of the Sahara Desert in Egypt

Crossing the great Nile River north of Luxor

Ancient ruins of Dendara from the late Egyptian dynasties

In the old Medina of Tunis, Tunisia

In the modern downtown of Casablanca, Morocco

Strong Portuguese influences seen in Praia, Cape Verde Republic

Fish for dinner in Porto Novo, Cape Verde Republic

Fishermen's boats beached along the shore of Dakar, Senegal

Fishermen of Sekondi, Ghana

The colorful marketplace in Takoradi, Ghana

In the highlands of Kenya, (Work of Chris 73, CC BY SA 3.0, Wikimedia.org)

The Maasai of Kenya, proud warriors and cattlemen, (Work of Harvey Barrison, CC BY SA 2.0, Wikimedia.org)

Fishermen on Lake Victoria – Africa's greatest lake

Victoria Falls, the greatest cataract in the world

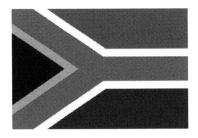

THE REPUBLIC OF SOUTH AFRICA

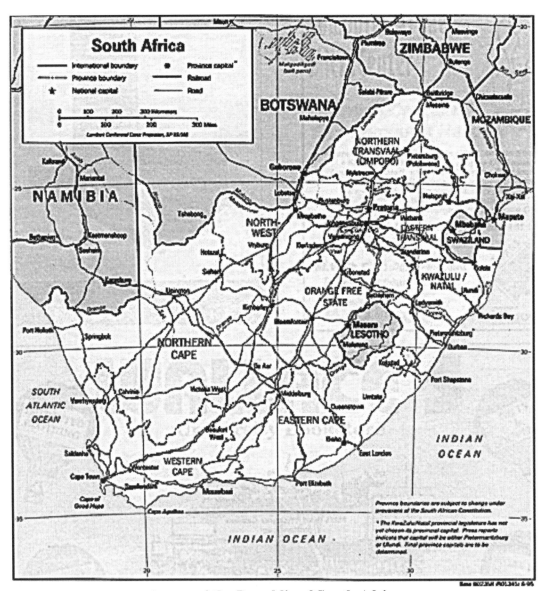

A map of the Republic of South Africa

The Republic of South Africa is without question one of the world's most dramatic and beautiful countries. Situated at the bottom of the African continent, it is a land guarded by two oceans, the Atlantic on the west and the Indian Ocean bordering the south and east coast.

Most of South Africa sits above the cliffs and mountains that wrap around its western, southern and eastern shores, giving the country a landscape of breathtaking vistas.

South Africa is a large country, occupying 1,221,043 square kilometers or 471,443 square miles. By comparison, this makes it the size of France, Spain and Portugal combined. The national population is just over 54,000,000, but by European standards it is not overly populated. Unlike most other Sub Saharan countries, South Africa is quite mixed when it comes to ethnic composition. The bulk of the population, 79.2 percent is Black African, often referred to locally as Bantu, the two largest national groups being the Xhosa and Zulu. The European population accounts for 8.9 percent, primarily a mix of Dutch Afrikaans and English, but with other immigrant groups making up a small percentage. There is a group called Cape Coloured accounting for 8.9 percent of the population. These are people of mixed European, African and Indian heritage from the days before strict segregation under the Apartheid laws. The Asian population is 2.5 percent, but the vast majority are descendants of Indians who were brought over by the British to work in the sugar cane fields of what was then Natal Province.

The government is democratic with an elected legislature and president. South Africa is a member of the British Commonwealth of Nations, but it does not accept the British crown as its own, preferring the republican status, which some other Commonwealth nations have also adopted. This decision was by referendum back in 1961 when only Europeans were able to vote. Because of its strong racial policy known as Apartheid, the country was later pressured into leaving the British Commonwealth of Nations, but it was permitted to reenter in 1994 after holding its first universal election with the end of Apartheid.

The transition from a system of strict racial segregation that was implemented in 1948 was peaceful as both the white dominated government and the African National Congress led by Nelson Mandela negotiated the terms of the first free election in which all citizens could participate. At the time most world nations had predicted that the country would plunge into a civil war along ethnic or racial lines before it would ever stand a chance of emerging from Apartheid. It came as a great surprise to the world that this did not happen. Today the country struggles with high unemployment, a slowly rising Black middle class and a slowly rising white impoverished class. The government has attempted to establish a policy of redistribution of some of the nation's wealth, building homes for the poor and stabilizing the economy. Fortunately for South Africa, the ANC (African National Congress) under Nelson Mandela and with the encouragement of Bishop Desmond Tutu established a Commission of Truth and Reconciliation insuring that the European population did not voluntarily flee or be forced out of the country, as has been true in neighboring Zimbabwe, the former Southern Rhodesia. It has been a successful policy and today the European population is moderately content to be a fully integrated and vital part of the national economy and political system. But whites worry that various factions within the ANC are agitating to divest whites of some of their land and wealth. Mandela preached a policy of not forgetting the indignities and atrocities of Apartheid, but combined with total forgiveness has been a cornerstone of South Africa's success. Hopefully his teachings will not fall to the pressure of this new movement. And among the younger generation there is more of a feeling of racial harmony that could even become an example for the United States, which still struggles with the concept.

THE NATURAL LANDSCAPE: I could use numerous adjectives to describe the natural landscape of South Africa, but none would be adequate to convey the true extent and power of the scenery. This is a country of superlatives. Yet it is a somewhat harsh land in that more than half of the nation is arid to semi-arid, but with many sources of irrigation even the drier areas of the country have been productive. South Africa has both climatic and biotic diversity that gives the people a great potential in the raising of a variety of crops to fulfill most needs. Likewise the diversity provides the people with an abundance of natural regions for recreational purposes and in today's realm of tourism, this is a highly marketable commodity.

Most of South Africa is situated above the Great Escarpment that completely encircles the country just inland from the coastline. In the west and southwest this escarpment reaches its greatest heights. It is a line of cliffs that rises to a maximum elevation of just over 1,000 meters or 3,300 feet. The edge of the Great Escarpment is spectacular, similar in nature to Arizona's Mogollon Rim that marks the edge of the Colorado Plateau. Above the Great Escarpment is the Karoo, a semi-arid grassland or scrubland that merges to the north and east with the wetter grassland of the Veld. The Karoo was difficult for early settlers to penetrate, as the land is ribbed with rugged outcrops that made early wagon travel precarious.

The region of Cape Town is where the Swartberg Mountains contain sheltered valleys that have a mild Mediterranean climate. Here wet winters and dry summers, with reliable rainfall of around 510 millimeters or 20 inches per year creates a condition in which grapes thrive. This is the heart of the wine-producing region. The Cape Peninsula is part of the Cape Fold Mountains, dominated over by the flat-topped Table Mountain, one of the great landmarks of the country. Here the peninsula juts into the sea, creating the boundary between Atlantic and Indian Ocean waters even though in reality all the oceans of the world are intermingled as one great body of water.

As you travel north from the Cape Region, the land dries out and becomes the Kalahari Desert with the even drier Namib Desert along the coast. The Kalahari is good for cattle ranching, but it is the emptiest part of South Africa, as it was not the most favored locale in which to settle. Life in the Kalahari, like parts of the American Southwest, was difficult to colonize and still is to this day.

The escarpment continues eastward along the Indian Ocean, running parallel to a series of coastal ranges known as the Cape Fold Mountains, and they combine to create some spectacular landscapes in what is called the Garden Route. Between the coastal mountains and the Great Escarpment is a semi-arid plateau often called the Lesser Karoo where there are numerous green valleys tucked into the folds of the escarpment. If when cruising along the coast your cruise line offers any tours into the Lesser Karoo to visit a game park, I would highly recommend it for the majesty of its scenery.

Eventually the escarpment meets the Drakensburg; a sharply uplifted escarpment that gives the appearance of being a mountain range, but in reality is not. It contains many layers of sedimentary rock that dip northward and have been eroded by fast flowing rivers that flow to the Orange River. The highest elevation, which is the "roof of South Africa," reaches 3,482 meters or 11,424 feet above sea level. When winter storms cross these mountains, precipitation falls as snow, the only region in the country that regularly has temperatures cold enough. Many of the rock layers within the Drakensberg date back to nearly 200 million years. It was the early Dutch settlers that saw the escarpment edge as the spine of a dragon, and thus in Afrikaans the name Drakensburg or dragon's mountains. If when visiting Durban on your cruise that a tour into the Drakensburg is offered, it would afford an opportunity to see the most spectacular of all scenic landscapes in South Africa.

The interior of South Africa dips gently from the escarpment to the north, drained by the Orange River and its many tributaries. The Limpopo River drains the northern plateau to the Indian Ocean. This high plateau that varies from nearly 2,130 meters or 7,000 feet to as low as 1,000 meters or 3,300 feet is covered in rich grass to the south and a mix of grass and scrub woodland to the north. It is the heartland of South Africa, home to an extensive ranching and dry farming economy combined with mining. Gold and diamonds brought great wealth to the interior, the land simply known as the Veld. It is vast and essentially flat to gently rolling, a land in which the sky overhead appears to dominate. There is a haunting beauty to the Veld. In the northeast where human settlement was not as extensive you currently find most of the wildlife preserves. The most famous of South Africa's parks is Kruger National Park, one of Africa's premier wildlife reserves. Many cruise lines offer either a pre or post cruise land excursion to Kruger and this is definitely a highlight of any visit to the interior.

Warm ocean currents wash the eastern coast of South Africa. This encourages large quantities of moisture to uplift along the spine of the Drakensburg, creating a humid environment cloaked in thick woodland and forest. With a warm climate, this is the greenest and most well-watered part of the country. It was here that early settlers found they could raise sugar cane, tea and other tropical luxury plantation crops. The far northeastern corner of the coastal region is not well settled, and here you again find several game parks. The land in this region is exceptionally humid and has in the past been a region in which malaria was a factor in limiting settlement.

South Africa is noted for its numerous game parks, as the country has set aside vast tracts of land in which the native animal life can roam. There are elephants, giraffes, zebra, lions, cheetah and leopards plus many prey animals such as gazelle, wildebeest and numerous others. Despite a large population, there has always been recognition of the value of preservation, and today this is a major tourist draw. The game parks all offer excellent accommodation, much of it in the five-star category.

The plant life is equally diverse with thousands of species that include grasses, small shrubs and woodlands. The country is not heavily endowed with forests because of it essentially being a drier landscape than the tropical lands to the north. What forests once thrived were decimated by deforestation and today there are strong conservation measures to restore many areas. The wildlife was also decimated during the 18th and 19th centuries, but today's recognition of the value of preservation has brought about greater enlightenment despite a growing population and agricultural/urban expansion. Poaching does occur in the parks, but it is not as severe as in the poorer countries such as Kenya, Tanzania and Uganda. The greatest danger has been to the rhino because of the high demand for its horn in eastern Asia. In this case poaching is not for "bush" meat but rather for pure financial gain.

It is believed that if global warming continues, South Africa will face both higher temperatures and less precipitation. Droughts have increased in recent years, and this is of major concern. As a semi-arid nation any slight increase in overall temperature could have a devastating impact upon the amount of rainfall and this could translate into an economic disaster.

CULTURAL DIVERSITY: As noted previously, South Africa is a country where there are distinct ethnic differences, but with the Black African population dominating in numbers. But the major racial categories noted earlier do not tell the whole story. This is a country where the traditional racial divisions do not account for all of the diversity.

Like the United States, South Africa has an illegal immigration problem. The largest percentage comes from Zimbabwe because of that country's political and economic turmoil. There numbers are followed by a large illegal influx from the Democratic Republic of Congo, again for the same reasons. Within the South African Black African population, there are many distinct tribal groups that still maintain strong cultural identity even though most live in urban centers and normally participate in work and play as one community.

In the western half of the country the Xhosa people are the major ethnic group, still keeping many of their language and customs alive. In the eastern half of the country, the Zulu, once mighty warriors, maintain their language and social customs. The eastern coastal province is known as KwaZulu-Natal and Durban's airport is King Shaka International, named in honor of the great Zulu king of the mid 19th century. In the north, people we should properly identify as San and Khoikhoi are the predominant ethnic groups. These names may be unfamiliar; Europeans knew them as the Bushmen and Hottentot peoples.

South Africa is essentially today a Christian nation, but with many Protestant sects along with Roman Catholics. Islamic people make up less than 1.5 percent of the population while Hindu account for 1.2 percent and Jews only make up 0.2 percent. The Islamic and Hindu faiths are found primarily in the Cape Town and Durban regions where East Indian settlers were brought over by the British in the mid 19th century to work in agricultural pursuits. Traditional tribal religions are practiced by a very small minority, but often along with Christianity. Traditional African healing still plays a role among many Black Africans even though modern medical services are available.

Officially South Africa is a multilingual country. The two primary languages are English and Afrikaans, but there are nine other native tongues that are also recognized as national languages. Two of the most dominant are Xhosa and Zulu. The South African national anthem is actually sung in Xhosa, Zulu, Afrikaans and ends in English. It is considered to be one of the world's two most beautiful, the other being New Zealand, which is sung in Maori and English. There are numerous other languages spoken in the country, representing smaller tribal groups and immigrants, both legal and illegal. Throughout the country you will find information sighs written in English and Afrikaans, as the two dominant languages. You will also notice this on the banknotes. In the eastern part of the country you will find signs written in Zulu as well.

GOVERNMENT: South Africa is somewhat unique in that it is essentially a parliamentary republic. The president of the country is both head of state and head of the governing party. There is no prime minister, as is usual in parliamentary systems of government. That position was merged in to the president's role in 1984 when the constitution was rewritten.

The Constitution of South Africa is the supreme document that dictates all actions of the government, and it is the courts that have the final word as to legislative action being constitutional. The Parliament meets in Cape Town, and it is divided into two houses. The National Assembly has 400 seats, elected for five-year terms on a proportional basis. The National Council of Provinces is the upper house consisting of 90 members equally representing the nine provinces. The upper house also is based upon five-year terms of office.

The party holding the majority in the National Assembly selects the President from within its own, similar to the way prime ministers in other countries are appointed. But once selected, the President loses his seat in the National Assembly and is no longer a part of the legislative body. The President then chooses his Cabinet Ministers. But the National Assembly can remove a president or cabinet ministers through a vote of no confidence. Since the first free election in 1994, the African National Congress has held a majority in the National Assembly. The first president was Nelson Mandela, but he chose to serve for only one term. The next president was Jacob Zuma, serving in his second five-year term. But he was forced from power in early 2018 because of rampant corruption. The new president is Cyril Ramaphosa who is the leader of the African National Congress. He has pledged to clean up the corruption that has existed under Zuma's tenure. But promises and action are two different animals.

South Africa is unique among world nations in that it essentially has three national capital cities. The Parliament meets in Cape Town, but the executive offices of the president and cabinet ministers are in Pretoria, where foreign nations have their official embassies. The Supreme Court of Appeal of South Africa meets in Bloemfontein. So if anyone asks you what is the capital of South Africa, it is acceptable to say Pretoria since it has the majority of government departments and handles all international affairs.

Since universal voting in 1994, the Black African majority takes a very strong interest in the role of government. Protest marches or strikes have become quite commonplace, but unfortunately many have been met with strong police action. You may remember a miner's strike three years ago when the police opened fire and killed many of the protestors. Many claim that the government has become repressive even in spite of the Constitution. Although South Africa is one of the most democratic nations on the continent, it still has a problem with police action in the face of any civic demonstrations.

South Africa still has a relatively overall high crime rate, especially in urban areas and relating to property. Many middle class and upper income neighborhoods have private security patrols, and there are walls or fences surrounding many middle and upper income homes. The security business is quite large with nearly half a million security guards in service. As a visitor this is often a concern, but the precautions laid down in the introductory chapters should be followed, and you should have no problems. It is best to have a guide or driver accompany you on most outings just for that added measure of comfort. But do not let the warnings you read in all of the guidebooks deter you from getting out and enjoying the natural beauty and cultural diversity.

South Africa has a large and well-equipped military, known as the South African National Defence Force. Today it is fully integrated, having combined the former all white military with units from the major African nationalist forces. It is a highly trained and formidable force, but it does not involve itself in the internal affairs of the nation, as is true throughout most of Africa. The South African military has participated in United Nations peacekeeping efforts elsewhere on the continent.

South Africa was the only nation on the continent to have been nuclear. That is right when I say been. The country voluntarily dismantled its nuclear arsenal in 1991. The country is also a signatory of the Nuclear Non-Proliferation Treaty.

ECONOMY: No country in Africa has as diverse and dynamic an economy as South Africa. The GDP on a per capita basis is one of the highest on the continent despite the massive poverty that still exists. Since the end of Apartheid, the country hoped for greater foreign investment, but to date it has not been as expected.

South Africa does have an industrial infrastructure with the production of heavy metals, oil and chemical refining and the assembly of automobiles and most major machinery and appliances. There is also a sizeable light-manufacturing sector to the economy. Mining continues to play a major role with diamonds and gold being the two leading commodities. Most people immediately think of DeBeers when it comes to diamonds, and that is a correct association. DeBeers is one of the country's most important corporations and dominates the global diamond trade.

South Africa also has a thriving agricultural sector. It is a major grain and meat producer. The Cape Town region is noted for its fine quality wines. And the KwaZulu-Natal province is known for sugar cane, tea and coffee as well as a variety of tropical fruits.

This is also a high tech country with regard to all aspects of science. Medicine has been at the forefront, as noted earlier. Apart from cardiac surgery, the development of a yellow fever vaccine, x-ray tomography and other advancements in the medical field have brought several Nobel Prizes. There have also been advances in other scientific fields such as astronomy, optics and computers.

But despite the strong economic potential and the development of these various sectors, the non-white population has very high unemployment rates that in some cases are in the 25 percent range. Much of this is due to a lack of proper education and training. Even though education is available for everyone, many especially in the Black and Coloured communities do not have the understanding of the importance of gaining an education. And in part this results from family poverty combined with a lack of parental motivation to send their children to school. This is one of the limiting factors to the future growth of South Africa.

One important positive note is the emphasis upon good public education, if taken advantage of. In 2014, the graduation rate rose to a high of 85 percent for secondary students who achieved matriculation, a rate that was higher than in the United States. But this figure and comparable figures for more recent years do not account for the fact that there is a high dropout rate, especially among non-White groups. There have also been large numbers of students that receive first place standing in more than five subjects, a difficult accomplishment in any country, and many of them are from non-white communities. Once these levels were achieved only by white students in private schools, but today the overall national averages are based upon the total population in which the non-white races dominate. However, the dropout rate is still a strong negative in the South African educational system. The universities of South Africa were once segregated with the finest schools reserved for whites only. Today the universities are fully integrated.

The Cape Fold Mountains near Stellenbosch

Along the Atlantic coast on the Cape Peninsula

Flying over the Lesser Karoo en route to Johannesburg

Flying over the Highveld west of Johannesburg

On the Highveld west of Pretoria

Richards Bay in northern KwaZulu-Natal

Saturday at the V & A Waterfront in Cape Town

The major East Indian Mosque in Durban, KwaZulu-Natal

A wedding party in the Durban Botanical Garden for photos

Street merchants in Hillbrow, Johannesburg

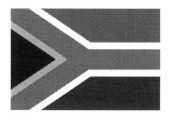

HISTORICAL SKETCH
OF SOUTH AFRICA

It is not possible to understand modern South Africa without having a brief historical background, especially to see how and when the hated Apartheid Laws came into being. Apartheid made South Africa a pariah nation, even forcing it to withdraw from the British Commonwealth of Nations and to be shunned by many countries. Its demise came as a great shock to the rest of the world, as scholars were so certain that the country would have a bloody race war before Apartheid would be dismantled.

PREHISTORIC PERIOD: Just west of Johannesburg is a UNESCO World Heritage Site called Cradle of Humankind. It is here that some of the oldest remains of humanoids have been found. There are several other sites around the country where early humanoid and modern human remains have been found. The country has been inhabited for approximately 3,000,000 years, making it archaeologically very significant.

Prior to being discovered and settled by Dutch and then British people, there was a migration of Black Africans coming south and taking up residence in what would become South Africa. Around 2,500 years ago, Bantu-speaking tribes began to settle in the Highveld, squeezing out the San and Koikhoi people. These people were primarily cattle herders and they had a limited knowledge of the use of iron. As the Bantu-speakers settled in various regions, they began to evolve into separate entities, the two most dominant being the Xhosa and Zulu.

EUROPEAN CONTACT: The first European to sail around the southwestern tip of Africa, sighting the Cape of Good Hope in 1488 was Bartolomeu Dias, a Portuguese explorer. Beset by storms, his journey around the cape proved that this was indeed a route to the East Indies, but one he deemed to be difficult. His original name for the cape was Cabo das Tormentas, the Cape of Storms. But King John II believed in a brighter outlook for the future and chose to rename it Cabo da Boa Esperança, what we now call the Cape of Good Hope. Despite being the first to discover the cape, the Portuguese did not establish a colonial base. It was not until 1652, that Jan van Riebeeck, a Dutch explorer established a resupply station underneath Table Mountain.

The Dutch set about establishing a thriving colony, bringing in slaves from the East Indies. But their expansion eastward along the coast and into the Cape Fold Mountains brought them into conflict with the Xhosa in a series of brutal engagements. The Dutch did manage to establish numerous towns in the valleys of the mountains, raising a variety of crops. Their whitewashed villages with distinctive facades and pitched roofs became the hallmark of architectural style that still dominates the region of the cape to the present. Many of the local place names like Stellenbosch, Swellendam and Paarl are still thriving communities to the present day.

When Napoleonic France invaded the Netherlands in 1795, the British captured Cape Town so as to prevent France from having access to this vital route to the east. But after the fall of Napoleon, the British return Cape Town to the Dutch in 1803. Soon, however, they recognized the value of this resupply stop with their now active colonization of Australia, and in 1806 they incorporated the Cape Town colony into the Empire. The Dutch had been expanding north and east into Xhosa territory and soon pushed out into Zulu and Sotho lands. Now the British hastened this outward expansion that ultimately led to three-way conflict between the Dutch (Boers), the natives and themselves.

Conflict with the British combined with a disdain for their way of living encouraged the Boer migrations deep into the Highveld where they established the new colony of the Orange Free State and later the Transvaal. They proclaimed these lands as their own republics, but that freedom would not last long. Greed over precious mineral wealth has a way of upsetting well-intentioned settlement. The discovery of diamonds in 1867 at Kimberley and gold in 1884 at Johannesburg brought many prospectors trades people and camp followers into Boer territory, totally upsetting their way of life. At the same time as the Dutch were settling, the Zulu were developing a powerful kingdom in what is now KwaZulu-Natal, impacting the tribes of the Highveld who with Zulu support were expanding their kingdom. Ultimately the ambitions of King Shaka and the British policy of expansion without regard for the native peoples created the Anglo-Zulu War of 1879. The Zulu had a massive army and used brilliant battle tactics, which resulted in a stunning major defeat for the British. But overwhelming weapons capabilities turned the tide and the Zulu were defeated. And with the death of King Shaka, they were not able to regroup.

The British had thought that it would be possible to build another confederation similar to that of Canada. But the resistance put up by Dutch Boers led to two major wars, the First Boer War between 1880 and 1881 and the Second Boer War between 1899 and 1902. British numbers included troops from Canada, Australia and New Zealand along with several colonial units. Ultimately the Boers were defeated and the Union of South Africa was created in 1910. And to add to the strength of the new nation, in 1918 the League of Nations granted trusteeship over the former German Southwest Africa. Ultimately South Africa incorporated it into their nation and it was not until 1990 that most of it became independent as the Republic of Namibia. The port of Walvis Bay was finally ceded to Namibia in 1994.

RACIAL SEPARATION: Almost immediately the Union of South Africa began to restrict Black Africans with regard to land ownership, tribal reserves and pass laws. The white population despite its British and Afrikaans differences did unite to a great degree, as both saw the Black African as the common threat to their high standard of living and political domination.

The year 1948 is the start of the passage of a set of laws that ultimately became known as Apartheid. The essence of Apartheid was complete separation of the races, but with white Europeans in control of the entire system. People were separated on the basis of skin color, hair color and facial features into four divisions - White, Coloured, Asian and Black African. At the time, whites constituted 20 percent of the total population, a figure that has declined to only 8.9 percent with lower birth rates than non-whites. To keep track of the non-white races, passes were required from birth onward. Housing was totally segregated with Black Africans relegated to living essentially in shanties in townships that were well removed from white areas. And strict curfew laws were in place to make certain that blacks were not out on the streets in the evening hours.

In 1961, white voters in South Africa chose narrowly to become a republic, giving up the British royal house as their own. Queen Elizabeth II lost the title as Queen of South Africa. A ceremonial presidency was established, but in 1983, Afrikaans President P. W. Botha merged the role of prime minister and president into one. President Botha was a very strong proponent of Apartheid and even strengthened many of its provisions. This led to the Commonwealth of Nations demanding that South Africa leave in 1961, not to be readmitted until Apartheid was ended. Many western powers initiated boycotts of South African goods, which drastically hurt the national economy.

Opposition to Apartheid began to fester, especially when the African National Congress advocated strikes and demonstrations. This led to stronger oppression and its most prominent leader; Nelson Mandela was imprisoned from 1962 to 1990. He became the symbol of resistance, which sometimes took violent form even though he was a strong advocate of peaceful protest. The police and military waged what amounted to warfare against many of the townships, leading to bloody clashes that could have escalated. But President F. W de Klerk transferred Mr. Mandela to a status of house arrest and ultimately began to negotiate with him a means of bringing universal suffrage to South Africa. Remember that President de Klerk was of Afrikaans background, yet he was able to recognize the need for ending a system of injustice that could no longer be tolerated abroad or by the black majority at home.

In 1994, the first universal free election was held, and given its physical majority, the Black African people elected Nelson Mandela as the country's first president chosen by all. President Mandela's victory over Apartheid was hailed worldwide. He was honored with the Nobel Peace Prize. South Africa was readmitted to the Commonwealth and trade embargos were lifted. Given his age, Mr. Mandela only served one five-year term, but remained as the great father figure for the nation until his death in late 2013. A man born to a Xhosa tribal family in Eastern Cape Province, he became an active opposition leader in the fight against Apartheid. He served 27 years in prison, was accused at time of being a terrorist or Communist, but ultimately became president. He also earned the respect of the white community for his pleas for national unity along with forgiveness. When he passed, the entire country mourned and he was given the largest and grandest funeral of any leader in the country's history. Today his portrait appears on every denomination of the South African Rand and there are portraits and statues of him throughout the country. Speaking ill of Mr. Mandela would be almost tantamount to treason. That is how beloved he became by the whole nation.

South Africa still has a long road ahead before there will be economic equality. Low wages and poor housing for blacks is still a major issue. The government is supposed to build adequate housing in the former townships, but the number built each year is far below what had been planned. Migrants and illegal immigrants have been made targets of black anger, believing that their presence takes away from the job market and available housing. Surprisingly the black community does not welcome blacks from other African countries, believing that their problems should not be brought to South Africa.

President Jacob Zuma who took office in 2010 has been accused of widespread corruption, yet the African National Congress won a majority in the 2014 election and appointed him president for a second term. It is hoped that his second term will be marked by more transparency and be beneficial to the masses.

World War I Monument at the Union Building in Pretoria

White and non-white entrances to the Apartheid Museum drive home a message

A 2008 official portrait of Nelson Mandela

TOURING AROUND CAPE TOWN

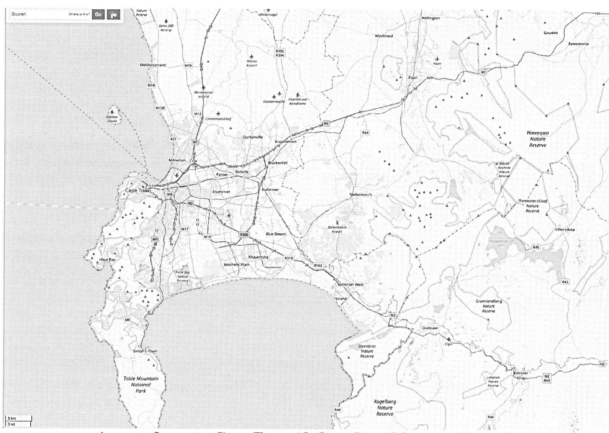

A map of greater Cape Town (© OpenStreetMap contributors)

Cape Town is considered to have one of the world's most beautiful natural settings, giving the city a sense of drama that is hard to rival. Most cruises to South Africa end in Cape Town, and cruises around the country's coastline normally both begin and end here. Thus for the vast majority of cruise passengers, Cape Town is the primary South African city they will visit. The largest urban complex is Johannesburg-Pretoria, but it is located inland approximately 1,610 kilometers or 1,000 miles northeast of Cape Town. And the vast majority of cruise ship passengers do not travel to Johannesburg, partly because of the distance and also as a result of so much negative press regarding its high rates of crime. Cape Town has a much higher overall standard of living, a larger percentage of its population being white or of mixed racial origins and it has escaped the ire of the press with regard to crime. Statistically Cape Town is not that much less violent a city than Johannesburg. But I must stress that as a tourist, if you stay in a good first class hotel and follow the precautions presented earlier, you will find Cape Town to be exceptionally enjoyable.

The heart of the city fronts on the Atlantic Ocean and is tucked into a bowl beneath Table Mountain, which is a world recognized natural landmark. This flat-topped mountain rises 0,006 meters or 3,300 nearly vertical feet above the city center. The mountain is the upper end of a range that is part of the Cape Fold Mountain complex, and it extends 40 kilometers or 25 miles south to the Cape of Good Hope. Lion's Head and Devil's Peak are the two accompanying mountains that complete this massive backdrop. Jutting north is Signal Hill, a lower mountain spur that separates the oceanfront suburbs from the downtown core. The bulk of the residential development of Cape Town extends east around the front of Table Mountain and out onto what is called the Cape Flats. This is an extensive plain that merges with the major mountain ranges of the Cape Fold complex to the east. The plain is the result of a slow rising of the sea floor over thousands of years. At one time the mountains of the Cape Peninsula stood offshore as an island.

The Cape Peninsula separates the cold waters of the Atlantic Ocean with the warm waters of the Indian Ocean. Descending air out of the Sub Tropical High pressure system that generally sits over the Cape Town region in summer causes warm, moist air to rise off the Indian Ocean. As it rises and cools, clouds form and then they drift over the top of Table Mountain and descend on the north face. This phenomenon is called "The Tablecloth" and is a distinctive feature that is quite beautiful, as veils of cloud drift down the mountain face and then evaporate. It appears exactly as if a tablecloth of cloud has been draped over the top of Table Mountain.

The climate of Cape Town is typically Mediterranean. Summers are dry and hot, yet tempered by the sea breezes, reaching into the 20's Celsius or mid 80's Fahrenheit on average. And there is very little chance for summer precipitation. Being in the Southern Hemisphere, summer is between December and March. During winter, storms blow in off the Atlantic Ocean, brought by the Westerly Winds. This is a cooler season with daytime highs in the teens Celsius or 50's and 60's Fahrenheit, with periodic blustery rain showers.

During 2017-18, Cape Town experienced a major drought and its few reservoirs nearly went totally dry. Water rationing was in effect and a major crisis loomed for the close to 4,000,000 residents of the metropolitan area. Fortunately the winter of 2018, which is the period of June to September, saw significant rainfall to officially end the drought. But now the city recognizes the need for better water storage and delivery infrastructure. And citizens have come to realize the need for better water use practices.

The landscape would normally be relatively barren on the Cape Flats with just scrub grass and low bushes. But since this area has been heavily populated, grass, flowers and trees are found in all upper and middle-income suburbs. The foothills of the Cape Peninsula Mountains are covered in thick woodlands, and many areas have been enhanced with the planting of many exotic trees in the high-end residential suburbs. But all of this extensive vegetation needs additional water, especially during the dry summer months. Some argue that all the additional vegetation does add moisture to the atmosphere and is not that hard on the water supply. In actuality, both arguments carry strength.

CAPE TOWN HISTORY: Cape Town is where South Africa as a Europeanized nation began. From the 16th century onward, ships from Portugal, France, Denmark, Netherlands and England would stop for fresh water and to trade with local natives for foodstuffs while en route to or from the East Indies. But it was ultimately the Dutch who established a permanent way station in 1652 that slowly grew into a significant colony. The Dutch did battle with the Xhosa over their attempts to extend their range into the eastern mountains. But despite numerous setbacks, several agricultural towns were established, raising fruits, potatoes, grains and vegetables both for subsistence, but also for trade with passing ships stopping to supply on the long journey to or from the East Indies. Being unwilling to work their farms directly, the Dutch imported slave labor from both Indonesia and Madagascar, a move that ultimately would create the Cape Coloured population that still is prevalent in the Cape Region to the present. It was during this period that the architectural pattern of whitewashed plaster walls with a sculptured roofline became established as the traditional design for Dutch houses and public buildings, a style still seen today as dominant in the Cape Region and not found elsewhere in the country.

When Napoleonic forces invaded the Netherlands, the British stepped in to occupy Cape Town to prevent it from falling under French control. Ultimately in 1814, the British and Dutch governments signed a treaty transferring control of the colony to Britain. Although the Dutch were granted a good measure of integration along with the British, there was a mass exodus, what is called the Trek inland. And as a result the Orange Free State and Transvaal republics were founded. But this dual colonial status would not last for too long. In 1867 diamonds were discovered in the Orange Free State at Kimberley. And in 1886 gold was discovered in the Witwatersrand fields that put Johannesburg on the map. And the influx of profit seekers brought great prosperity to Cape Town and swelled its population.

As noted previously, the discovery of precious stones and gold brought thousands of prospectors from many nations, and the tensions between the British and Dutch factions led to the two Boer Wars. The second war resulted in the creation of the Union of South Africa as a British Commonwealth Nation. But the Dutch National Party maintained a strong hold on the white voters and began implementation of the first racial segregation policies. In 1948, these policies came together as Apartheid, a hated set of laws that subjugated all non-white races until 1991.

Apartheid laws were very detrimental to Cape Town, as a modicum of racial tolerance had previously existed, especially between white and Cape Coloured. Near the city center was a multi-racial neighborhood called District Six. In 1965 with strict enforcement of Apartheid laws, 60,000 residents were forced to move and their homes, many of historic value, were destroyed. Because of the large colored population, they were given preferential treatment in employment, and a limited vote for national offices. But the Bantu (Black Africans) were forced to live on the fringes of Cape Town and held the most menial of jobs in the city. The Blacks were forced into townships and there were very strict curfew laws regarding their movement, especially at night. Because of economic stratification that has left most Blacks at the bottom of the economy, the townships that were established still exist today. Actually their populations are even larger than during Apartheid, but this is no longer a matter of racially forced residential living. One suburb known as Khayelitsha located southeast of the city may have as many as 1,000,000 residents who live mainly in shanties on dirt streets with few urban amenities.

It was off the coast of Cape Town that Nelson Mandela and other members of the African National Congress were imprisoned on Robben Island, and it was later in Cape Town that he gave his first speech as a free man. Thus the city has played a role in the abolishment of Apartheid and the establishment of universal suffrage. Today the city plays an active role in the national political scene because of both its being home to the National Parliament, but also its ability as a city to be more integrated socially.

Today Cape Town is a thriving city with a metropolitan population in excess of 3,740,000, a large percentage of whom is white (32 percent) or Cape Coloured. (44 percent), which are the highest percentages in the country. Likewise, overall the city has the highest living standard in South Africa, yet it still has remnants of former racially segregated townships. Khayelitcha is the largest former township, and it still has a population some say may be as high as 1,000,000, most of whom live in exceptionally low standard housing. There is a problem with drug use and juvenile gangs that prey not only upon the townships, but also cause problems of break in and looting citywide. Street crime does occur, but primarily at night. Yet there is a thriving nightlife in many of the restaurant and cafe districts, and walking is relatively safe. For the average tourist, it will not be easily visible that there is a significant crime rate in the city. Therefore do not be fearful of going out during the day on your own, or at night in small groups, sticking to the brightly lit main thoroughfares. The popular V & A Waterfront is one of the safest and most patronized of districts at night.

WHAT TO SEE AND DO: Cape Town is exceptionally spectacular with its mountain backdrop and magnificent beaches. But this is a big urban area that is quite spread out and public transport cannot take you to all of the important sights. Riding public transport into many areas, especially at night can be somewhat dangerous.

* Some cruise itineraries arrive in or depart from Cape Town a day before or after the actual cruise, and the ship offers guided tours of the city or the surrounding wine country. This is a good introduction for arriving passengers, but has less impact on those who have already stayed over prior to boarding the ship.
* Major hotels can arrange for guests to participate in group motor coach tours around Cape Town. There are numerous tour companies offering a variety of tours. You should check with the hotel concierge to arrange such a tour.

* For private car and driver/guide service you have three options. You can ask your cruise concierge to book it for you unless the ship is arriving and not allowing for a day of sightseeing before departure. If you are staying in a hotel, you can have the hotel concierge arrange a private car and driver/guide. Or you can check on line with Blacklane Limousine Service at *www.blacklane.com* for rates and booking information. A company known as Limousine Extreme offers exotic cars in their fleet and they provide very competent

driver/guides. Their web page is www.limousineextreme.co.za, which will detail their vehicles and services.

* City Sightseeing Cape Town offers what amounts to hop on hop off service. They offer five different quality levels of touring. For further information, check their web page at www.citysightseeing.co.za for further information on routes and booking.

* Blacklane Limousine also offers taxi service that you can book on line in advance. Or you can have your hotel arrange for a taxi with the company they prefer. Taxis can be used for sightseeing, but only if you arrange in advance. Do not negotiate with a taxi on the street for either transport or sightseeing, as you do not know what level of service and safety you will be receiving.d

* Uber does provide service in Cape Town and it is generally safe to use their service. I know it is a popular alternative, but I personally prefer either a private car and driver or a prearranged taxi through the hotel concierge.

* You do not want to attempt to drive on your own, as you may find yourself accidentally venturing into districts that are not all that safe. And you must remember that traffic in South Africa moves on the left side of the street, making it difficult for most North Americans and Europeans to adapt to.

The important sights in and around Cape Town not to be missed include (shown alphabetically):

* Beaches at Clifton - If you are looking for sun and surf, then choose any of the four beaches in the seaside suburb of Clifton, as they are magnificent, But you need to ask your hotel about the safety of the beach. And the hotel should arrange for a taxi there and back in advance.

* Camps Bay - This seaside suburb also has spectacular beaches, but it is also home to many great restaurants and bistros. This is one of the most beautiful beach communities you will see anywhere in the world. If you simply want to relax for a day and also have a nice meal, Camps Bay is perfect. But have your hotel arrange transportation there and back in advance. For more information on Camps Bay you should check out the following web page – www.cometocapetown.com.

* Cape Town Diamond Museum - The museum tells the story of South Africa's diamond mining industry, and it features an array of gems in different stages of finish. The museum is located on Level One of the Clock Tower and is open daily from 9 AM to 9 PM.

* Castle of Good Hope - This 17th century fortress in the heart of downtown Cape Town once protected the early colonial settlers. It is open daily from 9AM to 5 PM. Guided tours are offered daily at 10 AM, Noon, 2 PM, 3 PM and 4 PM. There is a canon firing daily at 10 AM 11 AM and Noon. The ceremonial guards have a key ceremony daily at 10 AM and Noon.

* Coastal drive to the Cape of Good Hope - This drive takes you through the most beautiful of seaside suburbs and beaches, finally into rather wild shoreline to the tip of the Cape Peninsula. This is where the waters of the Atlantic and Indian Oceans meet and is therefore a very important spot to visit. And the drive itself is exceptionally spectacular.

District Six Museum - District Six was destroyed under Apartheid laws in the early 1960's, but this museum brings that multi ethnic community back to life. The museum is at 25A Albertus Street set amid the colorful houses of the district. The museum is open from 9 AM to 4 PM Monday thru Saturday.

* Kirstenbosch Gardens - These magnificent gardens are a Cape Town treasure, tucked into the foothills on the eastern slopes of Table Mountain. Plan upon at least two hours to walk through the elegantly landscaped grounds. The vegetation is lush and exotic, as it represents the biosphere of South Africa. Free guided tours by tram are offered Monday thru Friday at 10 and 11 AM and 2 PM. On Saturday tours are offered at 10 AM. All tours begin at the Visitor's Centre at Gate 1.

* Khayelitscha or Langa Township - There are guided tours to enable you to visit either one of the townships that once existed during Apartheid. They no longer are townships by law, but still reflect the poverty and poor living conditions of the Apartheid era. And as a visitor, you are best off on a tour or with a private guide. The best tour operator is Imzu Tours, as they have over a 90 percent favorable rating from visitors. Their web page is *www.imzutours.co.za* .

* Long Street – Located in the city center, this street features some of the beautiful 19th century Victorian architecture that once characterized the entire downtown. Long Street is also a venue for many restaurants and clubs and it is a safe place in which to walk during the evening hours.

* Robben Island - It was on this prison island that Nelson Mandela and other members of the ANC were incarcerated. You can actually stand in the cell that Mr. Mandela occupied. Today it is a national shrine and one of the must see venues in all of South Africa. The best tour is to be found at *www.robben-island.co.za.* Visits are always dependent upon weather and sea conditions.

* South African Jewish Museum - Provides a fascinating history of the role of Jewish immigrants in the life of the country and in the diamond industry. It is located in the suburb of Gardens at 38 Hatfield Street. It is open Sunday thru Thursday from 10 AM to 5 PM, Friday only until 2 PM and closed Saturday.

* Two Oceans Aquarium - If you are interested in marine life, this aquarium features a variety of sea life from both the Atlantic and Indian Oceans. With different temperatures, the waters of each is home to very different species. The aquarium is open daily from 9:30 AM to 6 PM. It is located in the V & A Waterfront.

* University of Cape Town - For those interested in learning about the role of higher education in the country, the University of Cape Town is the most prestigious of all South Africa's universities. Once it was segregated, but today open to all who qualify based upon academics only. The university is in suburban Newlands. Tours are offered to visitors. To take a tour of the beautiful campus, e-mail a visitor request, which you get on line at www.utc.ac.za to visit@uct.ac.za.

* V & A Waterfront - This redeveloped shopping and entertainment complex is the highlight of the city center. It is a great place to sample local Cape Town cuisine, see street entertainers and mingle with the local people. It is one of the main attractions in the inner city. If your ship is docked for overnight, you may be right at the V & A Waterfront and then it is safe to walk at night on your own. The main mall within the waterfront center is open daily from 9 AM to 9 PM.

* View from atop Table Mountain - Reached by cable car, this is a spectacular view, but it is best to go in the morning before the cloud cover known as "The Tablecloth" forms. In summer when the tablecloth forms it creates fog and limited visibility from the top of the mountain.

* View from atop Signal Hill - For a closer and more intimate view of the heart of Cape Town, Signal Hill is an absolute must. You are still high above the city, but much closer than from Table Mountain and the perspective is totally different.

TOURS OUTSIDE OF CAPE TOWN: Every visitor to Cape Town should set aside one day to visit the magnificent wine country located east of the city in and around Stellenbosh. Even if you have toured wineries in California, the Mediterranean, Chile or Australia, the breathtaking nature of South Africa's wine country puts it at the top of the list. This is an all-day event, and you can do it as a group tour arranged either by your cruise line, hotel or with a private guide. Visiting Stellenbosh, Paarl and Franschhoek gives you a chance to explore a few of the wineries, have an elegant lunch at a winery and walk through parts of these small cities with their distinctive Dutch colonial architecture. No visit to Cape Town should be complete without a day in the wine country

To arrange for a wine country excursion, contact your hotel concierge to arrange a car and driver/guide and book lunch at one of the wineries. Or if you have already arranged for a private car and driver/guide, you can have the company with whom you have made your booking set up a tour. As an alternative, check on line with Kimkim, a company specializing in wine country touring. Their web page is www.kimkim.com. Another alternative is Tours by Locals. Their web page is www.toursbylocals.com.

The next chapter will focus upon touring the Cape Peninsula and the wine country outside of Cape Town with details on the various places to visit and where to dine.

* The Blue Train - If you are traveling to Pretoria, this is the ultimate experience. The Blue Train is said to be the most elegant train in the world. The rail journey takes around 26 hours and gives you a chance to pass through the Karoo and across the High Veld. Its sleeping

accommodations, food and service are equal to what you would expect in a five-star hotel. You should explore their web page to learn more about this incredible journey. The Blue Train web page is www.bluetrain.co.za. If Johannesburg is your final destination, it is a simple matter to have a limousine take you from the station in Pretoria to your hotel in Johannesburg. The Blue Train staff will arrange that for you. Travel time is approximately one hour or less.

DINING OUT IN CAPE TOWN: When you are staying in Cape Town or if you are only planning to spend one day while still on the ship, you will find that the city offers a great variety of restaurants in all price ranges and with a variety of ethnic traditions. Below I list a fine selection of top quality restaurants that represent the best in cuisine that features an African flavor or that specializes in seafood since Cape Town is an important fishing port. There is no way I can provide details on the hundreds of restaurants so I have chosen what I believe to be an excellent selection of Cape Town's finest.

Here are my choice listings for fine Cape Town dining shown in alphabetical order:

* African Café Restaurant – In the city center just steps from the Castle of Good Hope, this popular restaurant features African cuisine with an emphasis upon dishes that are representative of South Africa. Here you can sample the many flavors of South Africa, which are in many ways exotic, but yet still within our comfort zone. They are open Monday thru Saturday from 6 to 11 PM for dinner. Reservations are advised. And you should arrange for transportation there and back even if your hotel is a short distance away.

* Atlantic Grill – Located on the waterfront at Quay 6 in the Table Bay Hotel, this restaurant has an exceptional breakfast buffet. It is so close to the V & A Waterfront that if your ship is docked here, you can easily walk in minutes. They are open daily just for breakfast from 6:30 to 11 AM and feature European and African dishes in a dazzling buffet.

* Carla's – Located south of the city in Muizenberg at York Road, this is an excellent venue for early dinner if you are visiting the Cape Peninsula with a car and driver/guide. Carla's serves the freshest seafood and the style of preparation comes from neighboring Mozambique, giving you a distinct southern African touch. They are open from 5:30 to 10:30 PM Monday thru Saturday and reservations are advised.

* Cellars – Hohenort – Located in suburban Constantia, this elegant hotel with two dining facilities is one of the grandest and most elegant in all of South Africa. Of course you will need a car and driver arranged in advance to get there and back, something your hotel can arrange. The hotel has received a Michelin Star for its outstanding cuisine. The Greenhouse is a beautifully appointed dining room whose menu has an African touch. The Conservatory serves lighter fare in a garden setting. Reservations are a must for either dining room. The Greenhouse serves lunch Friday and Saturday from Noon to 2 PM. Dinner is served Tuesday thru Saturday from 6 to 9:30 PM. The Conservatory serves breakfast daily from 7 to 10:30 AM, lunch from Noon to 2:30 PM, afternoon tea from 3 to 5 PM and dinner from 6:30 to 9:30 PM. The hotel's gardens and the views of the back side of Table Mountain add a great degree of atmosphere to a visit to Hohenort.

* Chefs Warehouse – In the city center at 92 Bree Street, which is walking distance from most major hotels, but it is best to arrange transportation if going after dark. The cuisine is Mediterranean European and the menu quite diverse. The dishes are expertly prepared, beautifully presented. The service and atmosphere make for a perfect dining experience. You would feel as if you were dining somewhere on the French or Italian Riviera. Their hours of service are Monday thru Saturday Noon to 2:30 PM for lunch and Monday thru Friday from 4:30 to 8 PM for dinner. It is recommended that a table be booked for dinner.

* Lelapa – The Home – Located in suburban Langa, this is an exceptionally popular restaurant that will introduce you to the many flavors of South Africa. The best way to describe their diverse menu with dishes so beautifully prepared is to simply say you must go there or you will be missing a real taste treat. Their popularity rating is in the 90 percent range and that should say something. They are open daily from 11 AM to 8 PM, and for dinner a reservation is recommended. Langa is a fair distance from the city center, so you will need to arrange in advance for transportation there and back, which your hotel should be able to do.

* Miller's Thumb – This fine quality restaurant featuring traditional local cuisine and fresh seafood is located 10b Kloofnek Road in suburban Tamboerskloof, which is just south of the city center in the residential area below Table Mountain. You will need transportation arranged through your hotel, as it is too far for walking. Although seafood is dominant on the menu, meat lovers will find several dishes to their taste. Their menu features excellent choices in salads and main entrees all beautifully spiced to perfection. Reservations should be made in advance. Lunch is served Tuesday thru Friday from 12:30 to 2 PM and dinner is served Monday thru Saturday from 6:30 to 10:30 PM.

* Mount Nelson Hotel – The afternoon tea at this well-established five-star hotel is legendary in Cape Town. It should be a must on your list of dining establishments. Reservations are a must. You will need transportation, as the hotel is located at 76 Orange Street in the Garden District below Table Mountain. The setting is one of great elegance and the afternoon tea just dazzles with its wide array of teas accompanied by the traditional finger sandwiches, scones, cakes and pastries. The presentation and service meet the highest standards and even Her Majesty Queen Elizabeth would be pleased. There are two set times for tea, the first from 1:30 to 3 PM and the second from 3:30 to 5 PM.

* Mussel Monger and Oyster Bar – Located in Sea Cliff at 30 Regent Street, this great seafood restaurant is a short distance from the city center, but you will need to arrange transportation there and back to your hotel or the ship. It is a well-respected and popular place, and just as its name implies, mussels and oysters are the main menu items. They are open daily from 9:30 AM to 10 PM.

* Mzansi – This is a fine quality African restaurant located at 45 Hariem Avenue in the suburb of Langa. To reach this great restaurant have your hotel order a taxi and arrange for a pick up time. You need to make a reservation, as this is a popular spot despite it being located in what may seem to be a less than stellar neighborhood. There is only one seating

for dinner and it begins promptly at 7 PM. The menu features a range of traditional dishes found in the Black and Coloured kitchens of South Africa. And there is traditional music provided to compliment the meal. On weekdays they are open for lunch starting at Noon, but the dinner hour is 7 to 9 PM. On weekends they only serve the one dinner seating at 7 PM.

* Ocean Basket – This is a South African seafood chain of restaurants. The quality and freshness of the seafood and the sides available to make a complete meal are excellent. I have eaten at Ocean Basket restaurants in Cape Town, Port Elizabeth and Johannesburg and have always enjoyed the meal. The atmosphere is simple, and you are mingling with local South Africans rather than tourists. In Cape Town they are located at the V & A Waterfront, in Camps Bay, Plumstead, Sea Point, Table View and at Two Oceans Aquarium. Most visitors find the V & A Waterfront most convenient, and their hours are from 11 AM to 10 PM daily. I notice that their reviews are mixed, from excellent to not so good. I have very high standards and must add that I have never had a bad meal at any Ocean Basket. You get a good, fresh meal at very reasonable prices.

* Osteria Tarantino – This very excellent Italian restaurant is located just to the west of the central core at 125 Waterkant Road at the Cape Quarter Mall. Here is a chance to sample excellent Italian dishes as well as having vegetarian and vegan options on the menu. The cuisine, service and atmosphere are all top quality. They are open Monday thru Saturday from 1 to 9 PM. During daylight hours you can easily walk from the heart of town, but at night prearranged transport is a must.

* Signal Restaurant Waterfront – Conveniently located in the V & A Waterfront at the five-star Cape Grace Hotel, this fine dining establishment is at West Quay Road. Reservations should be made in advance. It is walking distance from where most cruise ships dock for their overnight stay. The diverse menu has a contemporary European and South African array of dishes that will suit a wide variety of tastes. The restaurant serves breakfast from 6:30 to 11 AM, lunch from 12:30 to 4:30 PM and dinner from 6:30 to 10:30 PM daily.

* Willoughby & Company – Conveniently located in the main mall of the V & A Waterfront, this is a very popular Japanese seafood restaurant featuring very fresh sushi along with a great variety of cooked dishes. The food is beautifully prepared and served and the atmosphere is quite congenial. They are open from Noon to 10:30 PM daily and if your ship is docked here and you are staying on board, it is safe to walk in the evening.

There are hundreds of restaurants from which to choose, but I have given you my personal selection of what I consider to be some of the best restaurants in Cape Town, primarily with a local flavor.

FINAL WORDS: I have visited Cape Town on many occasions. All I can add in conclusion is that this is one of the most beautiful settings for a city in the world. Cape Town, like all of urban South Africa, does have problems with poverty, high crime and social inequity. But despite these problems, the city has many beautiful neighborhoods, incredible beaches and there is an overall atmosphere of pride in the city and its surroundings. When visiting South

Africa, you must always keep in mind the fact that this country has only recently emerged for decades of intense racial segregation and discrimination. The country is slowly coming of age and will eventually conquer many of the ills that have beset it. Cape Town is the most racially and ethnically mixed city in the country, and it also has the greatest proportion of wealthy residents. In many ways it is unique to the country as a whole, yet at the same time it is very South African in flavor. I trust you will find it as enjoyable as I always have. If for no other reason, the natural beauty of its surroundings captivates all who come.

CAPE TOWN MAPS

THE CITY OF CAPE TOWN

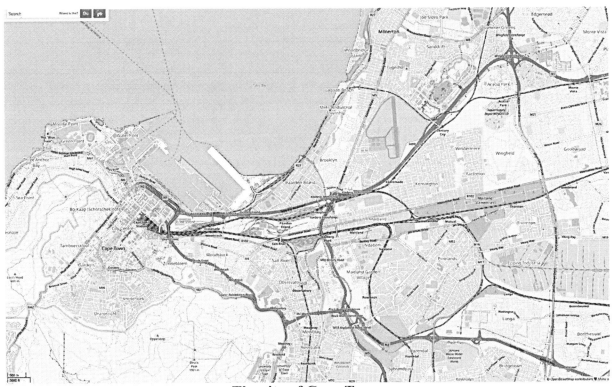

The city of Cape Town

This map is best viewed directly from OpenStreetMap.com on your personal device where it can be expanded or one specific area can be enlarged. Given the format of this book, it is impossible to display maps with the level of detail you might wish to have while actually out exploring the city. But the OpenStreetMap maps used directly are the tool I always rely upon.

THE DOWNTOWN OF CAPE TOWN

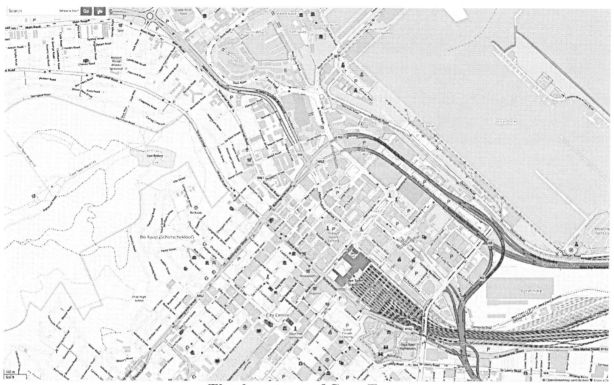

The downtown of Cape Town

This map is best viewed directly from OpenStreetMap.com on your personal device where it can be expanded or one specific area can be enlarged. Given the format of this book, it is impossible to display maps with the level of detail you might wish to have while actually out exploring the city. But the OpenStreetMap maps used directly are the tool I always rely upon.

THE CAMPS BAY SHORE

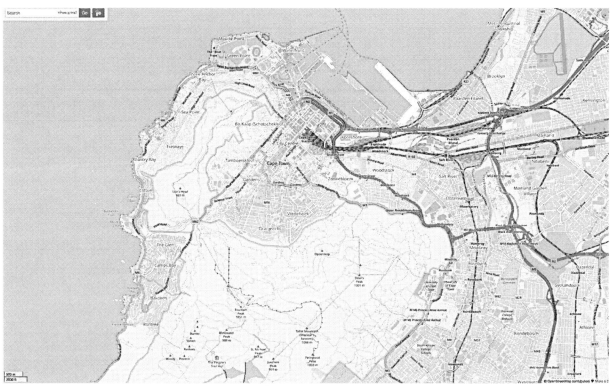

The Camps Bay shore

This map is best viewed directly from OpenStreetMap.com on your personal device where it can be expanded or one specific area can be enlarged. Given the format of this book, it is impossible to display maps with the level of detail you might wish to have while actually out exploring the city. But the OpenStreetMap maps used directly are the tool I always rely upon.

THE KIRSTENBOSCH GARDEN AREA

The Kirstenbosch Garden area

This map is best viewed directly from OpenStreetMap.com on your personal device where it can be expanded or one specific area can be enlarged. Given the format of this book, it is impossible to display maps with the level of detail you might wish to have while actually out exploring the city. But the OpenStreetMap maps used directly are the tool I always rely upon.

A view of Table Mountain just after takeoff from the Cape Town airport

Downtown Cape Town from Table Mountain, (Work of Christ Koerner, CC BY SA 2.0, Wikimedia.org)

Central Cape Town and Table Mountain on approach from the sea

Arriving in Cape Town Harbour

Adderley Street the great boulevard in the heart of downtown Cape Town

The Victorian architecture of Long Street

Long Street is filled with 19th century flavor

Parts of Adderley Street exhibit Victorian architecture

The Cape Town flea market opposite the City Hall

The South African National Parliament

Colorful Wales Street in the former District Six

Typical housing on the lower slopes of Table Mountain

A typical residential street in Tamboerskloof below Table Mountain

The Tablecloth spreading over Table Mountain on a summer afternoon

Cape Town University campus honoring the late Nelson Mandela

Suburban Newlands near Cape Town University

The Kirstenbosch Gardens below Table Mountain's eastern flank

Dutch colonial architecture at Constantia Hotel near Kirstenbosch Gardens

Victorian age Commuter rail station in Muizenberg

The High Street in far southern suburban Fish Hoek

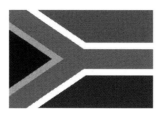

AROUND CAPE TOWN

Map showing famous Wine Country (© OpenStreetMap contributors)

Cape Town is more than just the city. It is an entire region that includes the vast urban sprawl, and beyond the city is the Cape Peninsula with its small beach enclaves and wild coastal scenery. To the southeast is the wine country tucked into the Cape Fold Mountains. One or two days in Cape Town is simply insufficient time in which to enjoy the beauty and soak in the flavor of the entire region. I know that when people are about to embark on a cruise they are eager to board the ship. If they have just disembarked from a cruise, most people are ready to fly home. With Cape Town being the primary port for embarkation or debarkation it is a shame if you do not take advantage of what it has to offer. As an urban center, it is the crown jewel of all Africa, so plan accordingly.

THE CAPE PENINSULA: It may be only a 40 kilometer or 25 miles to drive down the Cape Peninsula to the Cape of Good Hope. But do not let the distance deceive you. On average, without stopping, it would take approximately 1.5 hours to make the drive one way. Stopping to enjoy the many views, or to walk around in one or two of the seaside communities en route, you should plan on at least 2.5 hours to reach the Cape of Good Hope. Returning via

Muizenberg and Constantia, again allow at least 2.5 hours. If you include the Kirstenbosch Gardens and lunch, you will easily have an eight-hour day or more.

Starting out from central Cape Town, you will first pass through the heavily populated seaside suburbs of Three Anchors Bay and Sea Point. Although just a few blocks wide, this strip of mainly high-rise apartments and condominiums rounds Lion's head and starts you on the way to the Cape of Good Hope. The mountains of the peninsula come down to the sea with spurs of rugged country, often dropping straight into the water. The seaside suburbs are tucked into scalloped coves with white sandy beaches, but separated by mountain spurs. The first town is Bantry Bay with a mix of high and low-density housing. Then you enter Clifton, a large suburb with four separate beaches and very expensive homes and apartments literally clinging to the rocky sides of the mountain.

My favorite spot, and that of many locals, is Camps Bay. The suburb is built around a semicircular bay with rocky headlands and towering mountains just behind the main town with streets stretching upward as they extend back from the shore. The high street of Camps Bay is a good place to stop for light refreshment. On a warm day there are dozens of cafes that open their umbrellas and serve guests out of doors.

After leaving Camps Bay the main road travels along the shore through several small seaside towns, then it turns into the mountains and cuts across to magnificent Hout Bay, a popular crescent bay with a marina for small craft. From Hout Bay you pass through a toll station to now drive the Chapman's Peak Route with breathtaking scenery and numerous spots for incredible photographs. Then you emerge into a broad sand flat with the seemingly endless Noordhoek Beach. This almost deserted strip of pure white powder has tidal salt lagoons on its inside and the Atlantic lapping on its outer edge.

The road makes a loop around the salt flats and then your driver will choose either the less crowded, but slower Atlantic road (Route M65) or will cross the peninsula to the Indian Ocean side and continue south on Route M4, which is the busier route. Most drivers prefer the M4 drive.

False Bay is a broad arm of the Indian Ocean that was known in the 18th and 19th centuries for numerous shipwrecks, especially in the first few kilometers or miles, if you choose the Route M4. as you drive south to the Cape of Good Hope. Once again the mountains will form a dramatic backdrop, but this time on your right side with the Indian Ocean on your left side. And what will astonish you is the color change. The Atlantic Ocean along the peninsula is a deep azure while the water of the Indian Ocean appears to be a rich cobalt blue. This is the result of differences in water temperature and various forms of algae.

When the road reaches Smithswinkle Bay, it makes a loop around the marshy valley and the traverses high ground through the Cape of Good Hope Nature Reserve until alas it descends to the Two Oceans Restaurant where you can then find a walking trail to the lighthouse at Cape Point. The actual Cape of Good Hope is to the right about a mile distance via a nice walking trail. One question people ask is where does the Atlantic Ocean meet the Indian Ocean. And since the waters of the world's oceans are in essence one, it is we humans who have assigned names to the major oceanic basins. So there is no answer to the question. Simply put, west of the peninsula is the Atlantic Ocean and to the east is the Indian Ocean. And as I noted before, the water grades from a deep blue to the lighter cobalt shade. But exactly where the boundary is located has no real meaning in nature.

THE WINE COUNTRY: East of Cape Town, across the broad Cape Flats, the land rises into the many layers of the Cape Fold Mountains. In the valleys that are interspersed with the mountain ridges the climate is perfect for the growing of grapes and orchard fruits. The early Dutch colonists recognized this quite early and they began to settle, creating small farms where they raised a variety of fruits, vegetables and grains. Summers are dry, but not overly hot because of cooling breezes that do blow in from the ocean combined with the higher elevation of the valleys than the coastal flats. The soils are rich in the more alkaline nutrients that grapes thrive upon. Winters are cool and storms blowing in off the Atlantic bring gentle rains and snow to the higher mountain peaks. The snowmelt in spring then helps continue to water the fields through a series of irrigation works that date back to early Dutch settlers.

The colonists established towns such as Stellenbosch in 1679, Paarl in 1687 and Franschhoek in 1688. The town of Franschhoek was settled by French Huguenots who were given refuge back in the Netherlands and then who chose to migrate to South Africa. These towns are very rich in the historic whitewashed architecture of the Dutch colonial period. To the present, this architecture is revered and protected, as the bulk of the white population of these towns is of Afrikaner descent. The primary language of these communities is Afrikaans with English being a distant second. They began to produce wine when they discovered that the climate was so conducive to the raising of vines. Although Paarl has 115,000 residents, Stellenbosch is the better-known city with a population of 78,000. It is home to Stellenbosch University and serves as the major crossroads of the wine country. It is also surrounded by many wineries that have international reputations and offer tours, with many having five-star gourmet restaurants on site. If you travel to the wine country on a weekend or holiday, reservations for lunch are essential. And your hotel can provide you with a listing of the various restaurants and their menu selections. I will also make a few recommendations at the end of this chapter. I must admit that I have never found one that I did not find superb. The cuisine in most is a blend of European flavors with South African touches.

It pays to first stop in Stellenbosch and just take a walk through the city center. It is filled with beautiful examples of the Dutch colonial style of architecture, and in the spring and early summer there are flowers blooming almost everywhere. The city center has several churches that date back to the late 18th and early 19th centuries, and there are also small museums offering a historic look at the growth of the area. Most visitors continue on to Franschhoek, which has become a very popular tourist destination. It is a small city with an elegant high street filled with galleries and craft shops along with many cafes. And flowering jacaranda trees surrounds the local town hall and church. Most of the major wineries where tours are offered and where you can dine are found between the two cities. Fewer visitors drive north to Paarl, which is a shame because it also offers stunning scenery, wineries and historic architecture.

Here are the most significant attractions to consider for each of the three cities in the wine country (shown alphabetically):

FRANSCHHOEK:

* Franschhoek Pass - A scenic mountain drive to give you striking views of the valley and surrounding mountains. Even if the pass is out of the way, ask your driver to make sure you visit and enjoy the view.

* Huguenot Memorial Museum - Gives you the history of the founding of the town and surrounding valley by the Huguenot refugees who came via The Netherlands at the end of the 17th century. The museum is located in Franschhoek at 37 Posbus Street and it is open Monday thru Saturday from 9 AM to 5 PM and Sunday from 2 to 5 PM.

* Wine Tram. - A hop on hop off small train that takes you around the wine country outside of town. You can ride the tram from Franschhoek Square daily from 9:30 AM to 5 PM.

PAARL:

* Afrikaans Language Monument - An unusual piece of architecture with a tower that rises above the region. From the monument you can obtain dramatic views of the surrounding countryside. The monument is located on Gabemma Doordrift Street in Paarl. The monument is open daily from 8 AM to 4:45 PM.

* Bablylonstoren Gardens – Located along Route 45 halfway between Franschhoek and Paarl, these formal gardens displaying a wide variety of flora are quite beautiful and worthy of a walk, especially on a nice sunny day. The gardens occupy a property granted in 1692. In addition to the gardens, there are many 17th century examples of early Dutch colonial architecture. The gardens are open daily from 9 AM to 5 PM. Daily garden tours begin at 10 AM.

* Paarl Mountain Nature Reserve – This beautiful reserve contains the unique landform called Paarl Rocks and also a wide array of local vegetation, especially beautiful when the flowering plants bloom in the spring. The reserve is located off Jan Phillips Drive just west of the city center. Summer hours are from 7 AM to 7 PM daily.

STELLENBOSCH:

* Dutch Reformed Church - A dominant city landmark, this old church represents the very importance of religion in the 18th and 19th centuries among the Afrikaners.

* Jonkershoek Nature Reserve – Just on the edge of the city, a short hike through a natural setting where you can see some local wildlife adds a whole new dimension to visiting the wine country. Here you see what the land was like before settlement. No specific hours are shown, but the reserve is open daily during daylight hours.

* Rupert Museum – The museum is dedicated to local South African fine arts along with crafts, and it is located on Stellentia Road in the heart of the city. The collection contains paintings, tapestries and sculpture. It is open Monday thru Saturday from 10 AM to 4 PM.

* Stellenbosch Historical Museum - The predominant historical venue is located in the city center at 27 Rynveld Street. The museum contains artifacts and exhibits that chronicles the settlement of the region. It is open Monday thru Saturday from 9 AM to 5 PM and Sunday from 10 AM to 4 PM.

* University of Stellenbosch Botanical Gardens - Located in the city center, it is the oldest university botanical garden in the country. Although not large in size, this garden is devoted to both South African and European plant species. In the spring it is ablaze with blooms. The garden is open daily from 8 AM to 5 PM.

* Village Museum - Filled with local history

Whether you visit any of the major sights or simply enjoy the scenery, a trip to the wine country will enable you to visit one of South Africa's most magnificent regions.

DINING OUT: When visiting the Cape Peninsula most visitors tend to return to the city for lunch. And I have noted my choices in the southern part of the city that combine with a visit to the Cape of Good Hope to make for a full day.

In the Wine Country, the two cities that feature many fine wineries where you can enjoy a delicious meal paired with locally produced wines are Stellenbosch and Franchhoek. My choices, shown alphabetically, are as follows:

* Delaire Graff Estate Restaurant – Overlooking the vineyards high above Stellenbosch on Helshoogte Pass, this elegant winery restaurant is one of the gems of the Wine Country. Their gourmet menu is not very large, but each dish is elegantly prepared and presented. They offer lamb, beef and seafood combined with superb accompaniments. Lunch is served daily from Noon to 2 PM and dinner is available Wednesday thru Saturday from 6:30 to 9 PM.

* Delheim Winery Restaurant – Located on Knorhoek Road off Route 44, this fine winery dining establishment features a distinctive mix of African and European dishes paired with locally produced wines. The cuisine, service and view combine to produce a wonderful experience. Reservations are a must. They serve all three meals of the day from 9 AM to 5 PM.

* La Petit Colombe – In Franshhoek on Huguenot Road in the Le Quartier Francais Hotel, this is one of the finest dining establishments in the Wine Country. The cuisine is essentially French in style and is paired with excellent local wines. The restaurant does also offer vegetarian dishes. They serve lunch and dinner from Noon to 10 PM daily and reservations are advised.

* Orangerie at Le Lude – On Lambrechts Road in Franschhoek, this beautiful restaurant overlooks the vineyards with commanding views. The elegant cuisine is French, but the menu also features vegetarian dishes. The cuisine, service and ambiance are all outstanding. Lunch is served Tuesday thru Saturday from Noon to 3:30 PM and reservations are required.

* Restaurant at Clos Malverne – Located on Devon Valley Road, this is one of the finest restaurants set amid the vineyards where you can enjoy international gourmet meals paired with delicious accompanying wines. The cuisine is outstanding and the wine parings. And the combination of excellent service and sweeping views completes the overall experience. You must make reservations for lunch in advance. The hours of service are Tuesday thru Sunday from Noon to 4:30 PM.

* Rust en Vrede Restaurant – Located on Annandale Road, this is one of the most highly rated restaurants in Stellenbosch. The cuisine is exquisite, and the service and ambiance are superb. And each dish is expertly paired with the finest local wine. They are only open Tuesday thru Saturday from 6:20 to 10 PM, but if you are touring the Wine Country later in the day, this is an excellent choice for dinner. But reservations are necessary.

* Terroir Restaurant at the Kleine Salze Winery – Located outside of Stellenbosch on Strand Road, this is a popular restaurant with a garden patio overlooking the vineyards. Although it receives mixed reviews in the various ratings of wineries, I found the cuisine and service along with the overall ambiance to be excellent. Sometimes people over anticipate and then write bland or negative reviews. I consider myself to be sufficiently attuned to fine cuisine and I would highly recommend this venue when in the wine country. They are open Tuesday thru Saturday for lunch between Noon and 2:30 PM and Tuesday thru Saturday from 6 to 9 PM for dinner. Reservations should be made in advance.

FINAL WORDS: Visiting the Cape of Good Hope puts you at a point where two great oceans meet. Apart from the beautiful views combined with the knowledge that you are viewing two oceans simultaneously, you are doing so by still standing on terra firma. To visit the spot where the Atlantic and Pacific Oceans meet at Cape Horn, you most often only view it from out at sea. And most of the time the water is very rough. If you can go ashore, the weather is generally blustery. So here at the Cape of Good Hope you are able to enjoy this rare spectacle of two oceans meeting with weather conditions that are very mild.

No visit to Cape Town should be considered complete without spending a day in the Wine Country. I have visited the vineyards of Spain and Italy, those of Chile and California as well as the Barossa Valley of Australia. None of these other famous wine growing regions offer the absolutely breathtaking scenery of those outside of Cape Town. And this is the only wine growing region in the world where the cultural background is Dutch. Thus the region is unique and should not be missed.

WINE COUNTRY MAPS

THE STELLENBOSCH REGION

The Stellenbosch region

This map is best viewed directly from OpenStreetMap.com on your personal device where it can be expanded or one specific area can be enlarged. Given the format of this book, it is impossible to display maps with the level of detail you might wish to have while actually out exploring the city. But the OpenStreetMap maps used directly are the tool I always rely upon.

THE CITY OF STELLENBOSCH

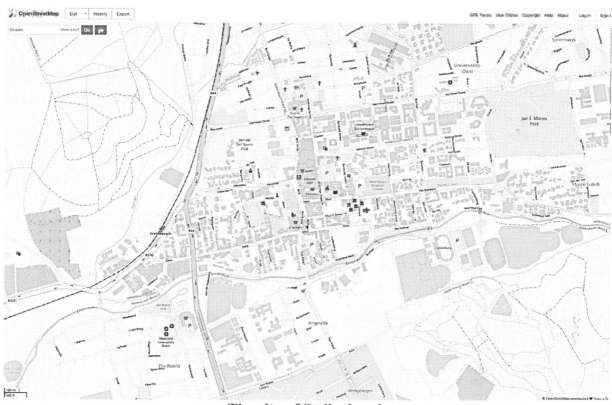

The city of Stellenbosch

This map is best viewed directly from OpenStreetMap.com on your personal device where it can be expanded or one specific area can be enlarged. Given the format of this book, it is impossible to display maps with the level of detail you might wish to have while actually out exploring the city. But the OpenStreetMap maps used directly are the tool I always rely upon.

THE CITY OF PAARL

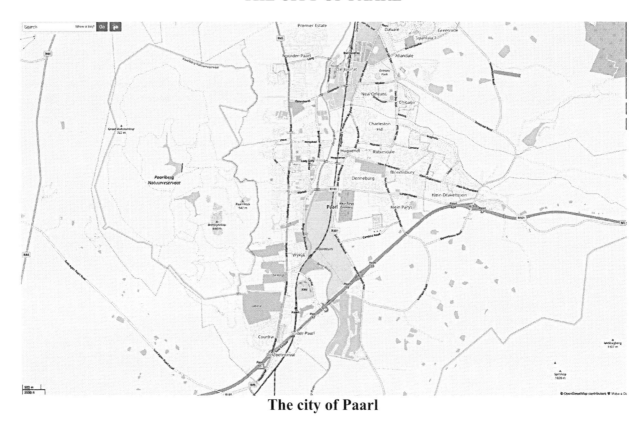

The city of Paarl

This map is best viewed directly from OpenStreetMap.com on your personal device where it can be expanded or one specific area can be enlarged. Given the format of this book, it is impossible to display maps with the level of detail you might wish to have while actually out exploring the city. But the OpenStreetMap maps used directly are the tool I always rely upon.

THE FRANSCHHOEK AREA

The Franschhoek Area

This map is best viewed directly from OpenStreetMap.com on your personal device where it can be expanded or one specific area can be enlarged. Given the format of this book, it is impossible to display maps with the level of detail you might wish to have while actually out exploring the city. But the OpenStreetMap maps used directly are the tool I always rely upon.

Sea Point from Signal Hill

Cliffside apartments in Clifton

Beautiful Camps Bay

High Street cafes of Camps Bay

On the beach at Camps Bay

View of Hout Bay

Nordhoek Beach with its long white strand

Elegant housing at Nordhoek

The Cape of Good Hope

Sign announcing the Cape of Good Hope, (Work of freestock.ca, CCBY SA3.0, Wikimedia.org)

The beauty of the Wine Country

The Wine Country beauty has no equal

Dutch Reformed Church in Stellenbosch

In the commercial center of Stellenbosch

The whitewashed architecture of Dutch Afrikaans Stellenbosch

On the road to Franschhoek

A village church outside of Franschhoek

The Dutch Reformed Church of Franschhoek

On the popular High Street of Franschhoek

At the Kleine Salze Winery in Stellenbosch

Gardens at the Kleine Salze Winery in Stellenbosch

Dining at the Kleine Salze Winery

On the way back to Cape Town

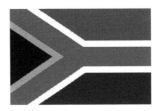

WHAT TO SEE AROUND MOSSEL BAY

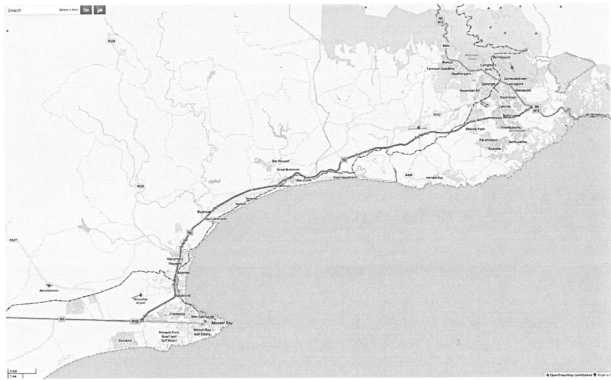

Map of Mossel Bay (© OpenStreetMap contributors)

East along the coast from Cape Town, the landscape becomes quite dramatic as the Cape Fold Mountains run parallel and close to the sea. The main highway east is known as the Garden Route because of the drama and spectacular nature of the scenery. The small city of Mossel Bay is approximately midway along the Garden Route between Cape Town and Port Elizabeth. This amounts to 388 kilometers or 241 miles traveling east of Cape Town. Many of the larger cruise vessels will bypass Mossel Bay because there is no anchorage for cruise ships in its small and enclosed harbor. Even the smaller luxury cruise ships anchor offshore and tender their guests to the shore opposite the city center. But if the sea is the least bit choppy, the operation of tender service becomes risky and the ship must bypass Mossel Bay and continue on. Unless you are traveling on one of these ships, in all likelihood you will not be stopping in Mossel Bay and this short chapter will be of little or no interest.

Mossel Bay is a relatively small coastal city with a population of only 60,000. This is still a community in which Afrikaans culture and language are very strong with more than half of the local population claiming it as their first language. The region surrounding Mossel Bay is an important farming area, which along with fishing and tourism make up the major sectors of the economy. Since 1969, natural gas has been drilled offshore and there is a small refinery on the edge of the city that adds significantly to the local payroll.

Most tourists who come to Mossel Bay are here for the beautiful beaches that spread both east and west along the coast where they can spend quite holidays away from the more popular major resort areas. This area is slightly wetter than the Cape Town region, as the warm Agulhas Current is a major influence. Evaporation causes moist plumes of air to rise along the mountain edge, and most precipitation still comes during the winter months. During summer, the city's population can at times double with the number of tourists visiting.

There is also very beautiful scenery both along the Garden Route and inland over the Outeniqua Mountains in the valley where the town of Oudtshoorn is located. The smaller cruise lines generally offer a half-day scenic drive to Oudtshoorn primarily for the grand views that are afforded along with a chance to visit a region that is inland from the coast and has a totally different character.

Unlike Cape Town, Mossel Bay has a more humid climate that would not be considered as being Mediterranean. This means that the summers do experience periodic rainfall whereas Cape Town is exceptionally dry during summer. Temperature wise, Mossel Bay is similar to Cape Town with a mild, temperate climate. On occasion there may be a chilly morning or even one in which there is a touch of frost.

BRIEF HISTORY: This is an old region with regard to human settlement, as archaeological finds show that modern hominids have lived in the area for over 160,000 years. Mossel Bay has the distinction of being the first place in South Africa where a European is known to have come onshore. Bartolomeu Dias rounded the Cape of Good Hope but never landed there. Rather he came onshore here at Mossel Bay on February 3, 1488. This is an important historic date for the nation. He did not do much exploring because of local hostility to these pale face strangers being in their territory. Another first came in 1497 when Portuguese explorer Vasco da Gama landed and exchanged goods with the local tribe, obtaining meat for his ongoing voyage. This is believed to be the first exchange between the native people and a European. In 1501 the expedition of Pedro d'Ataide came on shore after a major storm. Da Nova left a message tied in an old shoe to the branch of a tree, which was later found by João da Nova. The tree became a place where messages could be left and retrieved. This became an important stop for Portuguese navigating these waters for decades to come. Today there is a post office on the site and what is believed to be the original tree is an historic icon. The post office also uses a commemorative stamp that is highly valued by collectors.

The Portuguese never colonized any part of South Africa. Thus it was the Dutch, expanding out of the Cape Region that founded Mossel Bay in 1787, primarily as an excellent area for raising wheat. The town remained culturally Dutch despite the British takeover of the Cape Colony in the early 19th century. Incorporation as a municipality came in 1852. To this day the Afrikaner culture remains dominant, but the once strongly held views supporting apartheid

WHAT TO SEE: The city center is rather Victorian in architectural flavor, and the residential areas close by also reflect primarily 19th century architecture. Unlike the wine country, there are only a few remnants of Dutch colonial architecture.

* Apart from any tours offered by the cruise line, it does not pay to attempt to arrange for a private car and driver/guide, if it would even be possible.

* Smith Taxi is the main service provider in Mossel Bay. You can check out their web page at www.smithstaxi.co.za for rates and service availability. You can also book a taxi for sightseeing on line.

* Mossel Bay is too small to have any hop on hop off bus or local trolley service.

The few main sights of importance in the city are (shown alphabetically):

* **Bartolomeu Dias Museum** - This small museum and the famous post office tree of the Portuguese received mixed reviews depending upon one's interest in local history. It is worthy of a visit if you are staying in town and not going on a tour. It is located at 1 Market Street and is open daily from 9 AM to 3:45 PM.

* **Reed Valley Winery** – If you wish to sample some local wine and possibly make a purchase, this is the tasting room for a long established winery in Mossel Bay. It is located at R327, Hertbertsdale Road, but you will need transport there and back, so if this is something of interest, arrange for a taxi in advance. They are open daily from 10 AM to 4 PM and the drive there and back is quite enjoyable.

* **St. Blaize Trail** - This hiking trail along the outer St. Blaize Peninsula is very spectacular, but it is only for those who have the energy for such a nature walk. The views are spectacular, as are the steep drops to the ocean alongside the trail, and the views are quite breathtaking .The start for the trail is the Cape St. Blaize Lighthouse just off of Point Road to the west of the town center.

* **Santos Beach** – This beautiful broad beach is located just to the east of harbor breakwater. It is a popular sunbathing spot for locals and visitors alike. There are washroom and shower facilities and a restaurant adjacent to the beach. If you do spend the day enjoying the sun and sea, please remember that someone should always stay with your beach towel or other belongings at all times.

VISITING KNYSNA OR OUDTSHOORN: The resort town of Knysna is located farther east along the garden route, and it is a very popular destination. The drive is 105 kilometers or 65 miles and is quite scenic. Some cruise lines will offer a motor coach visit to Knysna, usually providing transportation and a guided talk, but upon arrival you have a few hours on your own to enjoy the lagoon and the waterfront shops and cafes. Knysna is actually quite a pretty town and definitely tourist oriented in contrast to the more historic, but less tourist friendly Mossel Bay.

If your visit to Mossel Bay is on one of the up market cruise lines such as Silversea or Regent, you may be offered an all-day excursion to Oudtshoorn, which is 87 kilometers or 54 miles over the coastal mountains into the interior. The route takes you over one or the other of two passes to Oudtshoorn - A dramatic route through the coastal mountains to the ranching town of Oudtshoorn, located in the Little or Kleine Karoo. This is a very scenic, but definitely winding route that should best be done on a tour coach if your ship offers it. Once in Oudtshoorn, most tours include a visit to one of the ostrich farms, as this is a major factor in the local economy

DINING OUT: If you go on any ship sponsored tour to Oudtshoorn or Knysna, chances are that lunch will be included. And in such a case, you do not have a choice of venue. But if you are staying in Mossel Bay, you may wish to have lunch locally rather than returning to the ship, which with tender service is quite time consuming. Here are my suggestions for the few best places to have lunch while in town, shown alphabetically:

* Café Gannet – In the heart of town at 1 Market Street, Old Post Tree Square, this more contemporary restaurant features local seafood with an excellent rendition of fish and chips. The menu also includes a variety of pizzas, hot entrees that include ostrich, beef and chicken along with vegetarian fare. An array of salads and sushi complete the menu. The restaurant is open daily from 7 AM to 10 PM.

* Carola Ann's – Located right in town at 1 Church Street, this small restaurant serves what can truly be called homemade dishes and also excellent baked goods. The menu is somewhat eclectic with a Middle East flavor, but also a local South African flavor as well. It is one of the nicest spots for breakfast or lunch. Their hours are weekdays from 8 AM to 4:30 PM and on Saturday from 8 AM to 1:30 PM.

* Transkaroo Restaurant – Located about 30-minute's drive east of Mossel Bay in Great Brak River, a trip here (by prearranged taxi) would be an experience in real South African dining because no ship guest will venture here unless reading this listing. This is a chance to see what a local South African restaurant catering to locals is like. The cuisine is outstanding and has the flavors of the region. The atmosphere and service are congenial and inviting along with the cuisine. And vegetarians are also welcome. Lunch is served Tuesday thru Saturday from Noon to 2:30 PM and on Sunday from Noon to 3 PM. Dinner is served Monday thru Saturday from 6 tp 8:30 PM.

FINAL WORDS: If your ship visits Mossel Bay it will give you an opportunity to visit a small coastal community with a strong Afrikaner flavor. And if your ship offers a tour into the Little or Kleine Karoo, this will be a chance to visit a small ranching and farming town on the edge of the arid interior as well as offering some awesome scenery.

THE CITY OF MOSSEL BAY

The city of Mossel Bay

This map is best viewed directly from OpenStreetMap.com on your personal device where it can be expanded or one specific area can be enlarged. Given the format of this book, it is impossible to display maps with the level of detail you might wish to have while actually out exploring the city. But the OpenStreetMap maps used directly are the tool I always rely upon.

Mossel Bay seen from offshore

The center of Mossel Bay (Work of Dewald Noeth, CC BY SA 2.0Wikimedia.org)

The beauty of the shoreline along the St. Blazie Trail, (Work of Satdee[Gill, CC BY SA 4.0. Wikimedia.org)

The waterfront and marina in Knysna

The dramatic route up from the coast to Oudtshoorn

Looking over Oudtshoorn (Work of thomas, CC BY SA 2.0, Wikimedia.org)

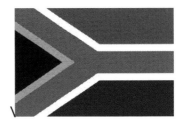

A VISIT TO PORT ELIZABETH

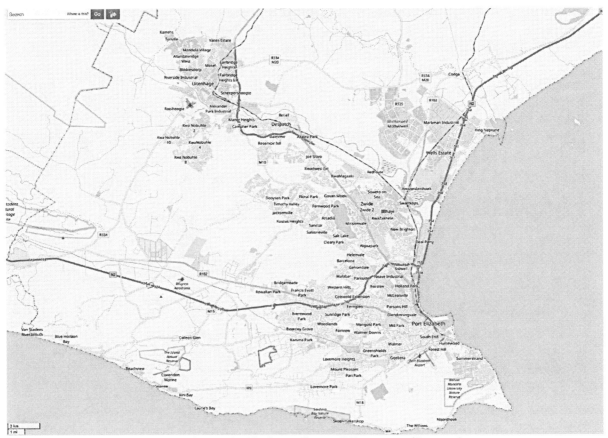

Port Elizabeth (© OpenStreetMap contributors)

Port Elizabeth is the largest city between Durban and Cape Town, and it is the capital of the Eastern Cape Province. The city population is 313,000 with over 1,000,000 in its immediate trade area. It is the center of a municipality that was recently renamed Nelson Mandela Bay in honor of the country's first president after Apartheid was abolished.

THE SETTING: By the time the Garden Route reaches Port Elizabeth, the climate has changed from Mediterranean to that of a humid sub-tropical regime. This means that temperatures are moderate during the winter and warm in summer, but there is much more humidity and rainfall than farther west. The mean annual rainfall is around 635 millimeters or 25 inches and there is some rain on approximately one out of every three days of the year. Most rain showers are brief and have a convectional nature, which means accompanied by lightning and thunder.

The Cape Fold Mountains that were close to the ocean now are located farther inland, leaving a gently undulating landscape of hills and valleys. There is a mix of grassland and forest, but much of the land has been cleared for farming and grazing. Fortunately many tracts have been set aside as game reserves and wilderness areas, the largest being the Baviaanskloof Wilderness Area, a very large park covering 485,622 hectares or 1,200,000 acres, making it the third largest such park in the country. It is noted for its scenic beauty and biodiversity less than for any big game animals.

HISTORIC SETTING: Port Elizabeth being farther east is less heavily Afrikaans, yet 40 percent of the local population claim the language and culture as their own. The city population is 33 percent English speaking with 37 percent of the population being of European origin. Among the Black Africans who comprise 31 percent of the population, 22 percent are of the Xhosa tribe. Nelson Mandela's home village is located in the interior of Eastern Cape, as the interior is the original Xhosa homeland.

There is a similarity in the early Portuguese history to that of Mossel Bay. Bartholomew Dias landed for water and supplies in 1488, Vasco da Gama noted the area in 1497 and numerous other Portuguese came ashore for water or supplies, but never established any settlements.

The Dutch, moving out of the Cape Colony, are the first to have established small settlements in the area. But it was not until 1799, during the Napoleonic Wars in Europe, that the British built an impressive fortress above what is now the city center. Their aim was to keep any French forces from landing since France had invaded the Netherlands.

In the period until 1821 there were no British settlers, and the Dutch had faced periods of warfare with the Xhosa in which there was one major massacre of over 500 people, including women and children. In 1820, in an attempt to secure the border with inland native peoples, a group of 4,000 British settlers arrived by sea from Cape Town. They began to settle what would become the city, naming it in honor of the wife of the then colonial governor of the Cape Colony. By 1873, the city was well established as a port for the diamond mines of Kimberley to the north, and a railway connected the diamond fields with the city.

During the Second Boer War many Afrikaans refugees moved out of the Orange Free State and into Port Elizabeth, adding to its Afrikaans cultural makeup. Given that the city's white population became more heavily Afrikaner, during the Apartheid Era, there were strong sentiments toward forced removal of black and colored people who had previously lived within the immediate urban community.

At the time of the first free election in 1994, Port Elizabeth was a city with a deteriorating central core, high unemployment, severe crime and a rise in HIV and AIDS among its black community. But the city has seen a remarkable turnaround in the past ten years. The creation of the Coega Industrial Development Zone and the infusion of foreign capital have brought nearly 50,000 jobs in manufacturing, especially in the assembly of automobiles. Today Port Elizabeth is the hub of the country's auto industry with Ford, General Motors and Volkswagen all assembled here. Given the agricultural hinterland, the city also processes a variety of food products for export and domestic consumption. And the port now handles a large tonnage of freight. The city core has made some comeback, and the Donkin Terrace and Fort Frederick sites are important venues visited by tourists. Most of the retail development, however, has taken place in the northern suburbs.

The city is home to St. George Cricket Oval where test matches are held. And the very impressive Nelson Mandela Bay Stadium was built to host several of the World Cup games in 2010. It is now used for a variety of sporting events, hosting local and national teams. It is the cornerstone of the city's sporting culture.

TOURISM: Port Elizabeth does have many services for visitors, and tourism plays a major role in the economy. There are several ways in which you can visit the major sites of tourist interest within the city, or take a trip into the hinterland to visit one of the game parks.

* Cruise ships that stop in Port Elizabeth dock close to the city center, and some will offer a shuttle either to the beach area where walking is quite safe, or to the downtown area where it the safety of visitors is questionable. And the majority of cruise lines do offer full day tours to a local game park with lunch generally included. These tours are well-organized, but do not always appeal to those who want more independence.

* Private cars with driver/guides can be reserved through your cruise line and the cost will vary with each company. If you find the cost not to your liking, you can contact *www.snupit.co.za* to check further into the two limo companies they list. It frankly does not look promising, as neither limo service shows any client reviews. I have always used the Silversea's car and driver/guide service and found the cost and service to be quite good. I would assume the other cruise lines use the same company, as Port Elizabeth is not that well supplied with limo services.

* There are car rental agencies, but I do not recommend that you drive on your own. Remember that in South Africa traffic moves on the left side of the street. And in any major city such as Port Elizabeth there are districts that you would not want to accidentally venture into.

* To hire a taxi for sightseeing, you can check on line for *Excellent* Cab Services at *www.excellentcabservices.co.za* or Airport Cabs on line at *www.airport-cabs.co.za* for rates and booking information.

* There is no regularly scheduled hop on hop off bus service in Port Elizabeth. In 2018, there was a limited winter service, but this is not a time when cruise ships are plying the waters around South Africa.

The major tourist venues within the city that are worth visiting include (shown alphabetically):

* Boardwalk Hotel and Casino Complex - A major hotel and entertainment complex along the beach in Summerstrand is an important part of the overall visitor experience. Some

cruise lines have their shuttle bus stop here at the casino complex, which is a very safe area in which to walk or take advantage of the beachfront. The hotel has numerous restaurants and the casino is quite lively and well-patronized.

* **Fort Frederick** – This is the British late 18th century fort, built in 1799, that was built to protect the coast from possible French attack during the Napoleonic Era. It is just a few blocks from Route 67 overlooking the city center. The fort is open to the public free of charge from sunrise to sunset on a daily basis.

* **Nelson Mandela Art Museum** - For a good sampling of contemporary South African art you should visit this museum at 1 Park Drive in the city center. The museum is open weekdays only from 9 AM to 5 PM, but closed Tuesday mornings before Noon.

* **Route 67** - This is a beautiful walk in the upper terrace section of the city center that includes the old townhouses of Donkin Terrace, many sculptures, the largest flag of South Africa and great views of the city. The walk is quite pleasant and gives you a chance to savor the 18th and 19th century architecture.

* **South African Air Force Museum** - For those who have a strong military aviation interest. One of the highlights is the flight simulator where you can try your hand at flying. The museum also has a good collection of vintage aircraft and helicopters along with many exhibits. You will need to have transportation to reach the museum, which is located on Forest Hill Drive in suburban Schoenmakerskop. It is open Monday thru Thursday from 8 AM to 3 PM, Saturday from 9 AM to 3 PM and Sunday from 10 AM to 4 PM.

* **South End Museum** – This local museum provides an excellent explanation of the history of the Port Elizabeth area. It also places emphasis upon the role of apartheid in the city's history. You will need transportation, as the museum is at Walmer and Homewood Roads in suburban South End. It is open from 9 AM to 4 PM weekdays and from 10 AM to 3 PM weekends.

* **Summerstrand** - This is the extensive beach area southeast of the city center that contains many new hotels, restaurants and shopping centers all lined up along a beautiful golden sand beach. The Boardwalk Hotel and Casino complex is the cornerstone of Summerstrand.

GAME PARKS: Around Port Elizabeth are numerous game reserves. It is difficult to get to one of these reserves on your own. So if your ship has any tours to one of the many reserves, and if wild African animals are what you want to see, then this is a must. These reserves are the best you will find within proximity to the ship in any of the ports of call. The major reserves include (shown alphabetically):

* **Addo Elephant National Park** - There is the main park well north of the city and a smaller division just a short drive northeast of Port Elizabeth. And of course as the name implies, this park is where you will see wild African elephants in their native habitat. Most cruise lines do offer a tour to the park. Trying to arrange for a visit on your own would be exceptionally difficult to coordinate.

* **Kragga Kamma Game Park** - This is a small game reserve just a short distance out of the city center to the southwest. This reserve is well managed and has brought together a great variety of African wildlife. in many ways it is more like a zoo, but still maintained in a quite natural setting. If your cruise line does not offer such a tour, you can have the ship's concierge book a car and driver/guide with the intent on visiting the park.

* **Shamwari Game Reserve** - This is considered to be the best game reserve within easy driving distance from the city. Located northeast of Port Elizabeth, here you will have a chance to see one or more of the so-called "big five" of Africa's game animals. And included are lions, the most sought after for those photos to take home. Most guests stay in one of the lodges for a few days, as in a short visit such as organized by the cruise line it is hard to know just how many animals you will see. But give it a try if your cruise line offers a tour for the day.

There are many other game reserves within a couple hours or less of Port Elizabeth, but visiting would normally require hiring a car and driver/guide and prior arrangements with the park in question. The three noted above are normally the ones that will have organized tours from the ship, and they are all three excellent choices.

DINING: If you go on a full day outing arranged by your cruise line, lunch will be included. But if you are staying in town and touring either with a car and driver/guide or taxi, here are my suggestions of top restaurants for lunch (shown alphabetically):

* **De Kelder Restaurant** – Located in Summerstrand at 39a Marine Drive, this restaurant has a broad menu of European and South African dishes including those to please vegetarians. The menu features a delicious array of starters, salads, soup, poultry, meat and seafood. In addition there are tempting lamb, venison and vegetarian dishes and numerous desserts. Lunch is served weekdays from Noon to 2:30 PM and dinner is served Monday thru Saturday from 6 to 10:30 PM.

* **Ginger** – A notable restaurant specializing in seafood, but also serving a wide array of meats, salads and vegetarian fare, Ginger is located along Marine Drive in Summerstrand and is accessible on foot if your ship shuttle stops at the Boardwalk Hotel and Casino. Lunch or dinner offers a delightful atmosphere, great service and beautifully prepared cuisine with an international flavor. They serve lunch daily from 11 AM to 3:30 PM and dinner from 6 to 10 PM.

* **Hacklewood Restaurant** – Well out into the suburbs at 152 Prospect Road in Walmer, you will need transportation to get here. This is an incredibly good restaurant that features a menu very much dominated by African flavors. The atmosphere of the stately house is Victorian and it offers a great degree of Old World elegance to compliment the fine menu. Reservations are advised. Lunch is served daily from Noon to 2 PM and dinner is served 7 to 10 PM daily.

* Muse Restaurant – Located at 1B Stanley Street near the city center, this outstanding restaurant serves European style food with a South African touch. The menu offers a wide array of starters, salads and mains. The menu is rich in chicken, lamb and beef along with vegetarian dishes. But seafood is conspicuously absent. The quality of the cuisine and service are both excellent. Hours of service are Tuesday thru Saturday Noon to 10 PM. Reservations at lunch are advised.

* Ocean Basket Brooks on the Bay – This member of the national Ocean Basket chain is located at Shop 2 Broks on the Bay, Beach Road in Humewood. It is an excellent choice for fresh seafood served in a warm, congenial atmosphere that caters to all tastes. It is a very popular national chain, and one of my personal favorites. The seafood is always fresh, well prepared and there are many tempting sides to compliment the meal. They are open dail from 11:30 AM to 10 PM.

* Shanna's Portuguese Restaurant – This fine restaurant with a strong emphasis upon fresh seafood is located in the suburbs on Circular Drive, Versailles Centre Lorraine, so you will need to have a car and driver/guide or use a taxi to dine here. The restaurant receives rave reviews from visitors and locals alike for its fresh content and distinctive Portuguese flavors. They serve dinner only from 6 to 9:30 PM, but many cruise ships do stay into the evening because of lengthy overland tours to game parks.

* This is Eat – Located on the harbor, this is a very popular local restaurant with especially good fish, much of it fried and served more in a fast food manner. They have a large outdoor patio overlooking the water. Fish and chips is a specialty and it is well prepared. They are open weekdays from 9:30 AM to 5:15 PM and weekends from 9 AM to 5:15 PM.

FINAL WORDS: Port Elizabeth as a city is relatively nice with its tree-shaded streets and bungalow type housing. Its suburbs are quite modern and possess all of the amenities found in Cape Town. The older, historic city center does offer a few venues of interest to visitors. And the Summerstrand beachfront is a very pleasant area in which to spend time and have a nice lunch. But the main focus on the day in Port Elizabeth is a visit to one of the game reserves, as organized by the cruise line. These trips are fascinating, but they do tax one's energy since they can be hot, dusty and the all-terrain vehicles are not very comfortable. I do not recommend these tours for anyone with back problems or who is of senior age since they can be tedious, yet at the same time quite exciting.

PORT ELIZABETH MAPS

THE CITY OF PORT ELIZABETH

The city of Port Elizabeth

This map is best viewed directly from OpenStreetMap.com on your personal device where it can be expanded or one specific area can be enlarged. Given the format of this book, it is impossible to display maps with the level of detail you might wish to have while actually out exploring the city. But the OpenStreetMap maps used directly are the tool I always rely upon.

THE CENTER OF PORT ELIZABETH

Central Port Elizabeth

This map is best viewed directly from OpenStreetMap.com on your personal device where it can be expanded or one specific area can be enlarged. Given the format of this book, it is impossible to display maps with the level of detail you might wish to have while actually out exploring the city. But the OpenStreetMap maps used directly are the tool I always rely upon.

Port Elizabeth skyline from the main expressway into the city center

The campanile in the heart of the city center

The old Victorian Town Hall of Port Elizabeth

The old Victorian Era row houses on Donkin Terrace

Donkin Terrace tribute to Nelson Mandela

Donkin Terrace mosaic along Route 67

The remains of Fort Frederick

The view over the city center from Fort Frederick

The famous Boardwalk Hotel & Casino complex

Grey High School noted for its soccer program

The Nelson Mandela Stadium built for the 2010 World Cup

St. George's Oval famous cricket venue

At Addo Elephant National Park (Work of Futuretec at Wikivoyage Shared)

Giraffes at Kragga Kamma Game Park (Work of NJR ZA, CC BY SA 3.0, Wikimedia.org)

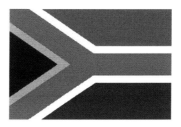

A BRIEF STOP IN EAST LONDON

Map of the East London area (© OpenStreetMap contributors)

East London, located in the Eastern Cape Province, is another port of call used only by the up-market cruise lines that present a more complete exploration of the coastline of South Africa. The city is not a major tourist destination and does not have the infrastructure to handle thousands of passengers that would disembark if the large cruise lines were to make this one of their stops. Only the smaller high-end cruise lines regularly include East London in their itinerary.

The city of East London has a metro area population of 267,000 of which 13 percent consider Afrikaans as their primary language while 21 percent claim English, but 62 percent speak Xhosa as the daily language. This is a city in which the European population is relatively small, numbering 16 percent to the Black African population of 70 percent. The remaining 14 percent is a mix of Coloured and Indian.

THE SETTING: East London is located where the Buffalo River meets the Indian Ocean, the river forming a deep estuary that is capable of serving as an excellent harbor. From the river, the city rises up onto a slight plateau that is gently undulating. The entire surrounding region is one of gently rolling hills, as the mountains are now farther inland and not as rugged as those that were seen along the Garden Route from Cape Town to Port Elizabeth.

The climate of East London can be classed as humid subtropical with precipitation occurring throughout the year, averaging 914 millimeters or 36 inches. As you travel east along the coast from the Cape Region, the climate becomes increasingly more humid, the result of the warm waters of the Indian Ocean supplying a steady supply of atmospheric moisture. Temperatures in East London can get relatively hot during the summer, reaching into the 30 degree Celsius or 90 degree Fahrenheit range. And humidity is also quite high, presenting a climate similar to that of the southeastern United States. Winter is relatively comfortable, but on occasion, cold air masses can blow up from the Antarctic, bringing chill winds and rain. And snow in East London has occurred twice since 1985, but only a small amount that melts relatively soon after falling.

HISTORIC SKETCH: Unlike the Cape Region, this area was settled much later, and by the British. East London dates to 1836 when it began to serve as a port, but located on the Buffalo River estuary rather than being directly on the ocean. The original town was located west of the river, aptly known today as West Town. The main heart of East London developed later on the high ground east of the river mouth. The port came to serve the military garrison located inland at King William's Town during the years of struggle with the Xhosa during the 19th century wars. To protect the port, a small garrison known as Fort Glamorgan was located on the western bank in 1847. Although the western bank served its role for military supplies and local trade, the actual construction of a port began on the eastern bank, which was the impetus for the main town to develop. The port opened for service in 1870 and with a rail connection inland, it was able to serve as an additional window to the world for the mines in Kimberley.

During the Apartheid years, East London found itself in a rather precarious position, as two of the so-called Bantu homelands nearly surrounded the city apart from its main road and rail connections. After the assassination of Steve Biko, one of the leaders against Apartheid, violence erupted and many thought it would flare into all-out war in this region in particular. Today there are no specified homelands, and with the end of Apartheid, there is growing racial harmony, especially thanks to the role of Nelson Mandela. A statue of Steve Biko can be found in front of the East London City Hall, something that could have never been thought of during the Apartheid Era.

Like Port Elizabeth, East London has become an important manufacturing center. And automobile assembly is the main producer of jobs and exports. Food products, clothing and pharmaceuticals all play a major role in the ongoing economic health of East London. This is in good measure to the creation of the East London Industrial Development Zone in 2004, helping to promote the West Bank as a thriving manufacturing area.

WHAT TO SEE: Tourism is not anywhere near as important as it is in Port Elizabeth. There are excellent beaches with very good surf in East London, and the young surfing public is among the main patrons of the beaches. Within the city there are no significant historic buildings or monuments to serve as a draw for visitors. There are a few small game reserves in the surrounding hinterland.

* If your ship stops in East London, tours will be organized into the interior to visit one or more game parks. But most cruise lines do not offer a tour of the city since there is so little of interest to visitors.

* Private cars and drivers can be arranged through your cruise line. Or you can go on line to East London Limousine Hire at www.booksouthafrica.travel/listings/east-london-limousine-hire for further information.

* Local taxi service in East London is not recommended.

* There are no hop on hop off bus services in East London.

These are the only significant highlights for your port call in East London (shown alphabetically) :

Duncan Village - Visit a residential community of around 100,000 that would have been an official township in the days of Apartheid. Only organized tours or private car and driver visits are possible, as otherwise you would be seen as an intruder by the local residents.

* East London Museum - It has a good collection of natural history items as well as exploring the cultural history of the area. The museum has a specimen of the coelacanth, the fish thought to have been extinct for millions of years. It also has the egg of the now extinct dodo bird. The museum is located at 319 Oxford Street in Belgravia and you would need a car and driver/guide to get there. It is open weekdays from 9 AM to 4 PM, Saturday from 9 AM to 1 PM and closed on Sunday.

* Floradale Center - This is one of the most popular venues, which is surprising to many to find that it is a shopping center that features regional fine arts and crafts. The center is open Monday thru Saturday from 8 AM to 5 PM and on Sunday from 9 AM to 4 PM. Many cruise lines use the center as a shuttle drop off point.

* Khaya La Banut Cultural Village - Located off the N2 express highway about 25 miles northeast of East London, this is a visitor center where you can learn about the Xhosa culture, music, dance and daily life. If your cruise line offers a city tour, this venue is sure to be a part of the tour. If you wish to go on your own, you will need a car and driver/guide. The center is open during daylight hours, but no specific hours are given.

GAME PARKS: These are the two major game parks outside of East London:

* **Inkwenkwezi Game Reserve** - Located east of the city, this reserve offers a chance to see many of the game animals minus the predators. The reserve also is known for its extensive bird species. Ships often offer a tour to this reserve. It is a short distance outside of East London, but to go on your own you will need private transport.

* **Mpongo Park Private Game Reserve** - Located within 30 minutes of the city, this private game reserve offers a less crowded opportunity to get close to some African wildlife. They have local guides who will take you out for a few hours of viewing in open vehicles that they provide. Many cruise itineraries offer this as a day trip if the ship is stopping in East London otherwise you need to have your own transportation.

This is a short list because there are no other venues in East London to recommend. Rather than take a shuttle bus to one of the shopping malls, generally offered by the cruise line, your day would be better spent on one of the excursions so that you learn something about the region's natural or cultural history.

DINING: Without having booked an all-day game park tour that will include lunch, you would need private transportation to dine out in East London since I do not feel the taxi service is the safest for visitors. For those able to tour around the city with a car and driver/guide these are my lunch recommendations for East London (shown alphabetically):

* **Bistro at Coast Wellness Centre** – Located on St. Helena Road at Espirit House, this restaurant features fresh cuisine prepared in a variety of styles, including typically South African dishes. And they have excellent desserts and baked goods served with great coffee and tea. Their portions are quite large and often as much as you might want dessert, there is no room left. They are open weekdays from 7:30 AM to 4 PM, but on Wednesday they do not open until 8 AM.

* **Grazia Fine Food and Wine** – On the waterfront at Beach Front Road, Upper Esplanade, this restaurant has a good reputation for seafood prepared in the Italian Mediterranean style. Although not representative of local cuisine, you will be able to have a good, fresh lunch that is well-prepared and nicely served. Their hours are Tuesday thru Saturday from Noon to 10:30 PM. On Sunday and Monday they are open from Noon to 10 PM.

* **Ocean Basket Vincent Park East London** – The ever popular Ocean Basket is here in East London on Avenue Street. This great family style seafood restaurant in East London lives up to the overall quality of all Ocean Basket restaurants across South Africa. It is open Sunday thru Thursday from 11:30 AM to 9 PM and on Friday and Saturday it remains open until 10 PM.

* **Table 58 Brewing** – Located on Maind Road, shop number 4 in East London, this combined restaurant and pub has a fine local reputation. They offer many traditional South African dishes combined with their own home brewed varieties of beer. During nice weather you have your choice of dining indoors or on their large deck with a delightful woodland

atmosphere. Their hours of service are Tuesday Noon to 7 PM, Wednesday thru Friday from 11 Am to 10 PM, Saturday from 10 AM to 10 PM and Sunday from 10 AM to 7 PM.

FINAL WORDS: East London is a port of call on just a few itineraries, mainly those of the upmarket cruise lines. This is a rather typical small regional center and representative of the cities along the coast with mixed populations with regard to racial and ethnic backgrounds. There is not much to offer the foreign visitor in East London, but once again as in Port Elizabeth it is the game parks in the surrounding countryside that are the major draw that bring cruise ships into port. I highly recommend a tour to one of the game parks unless physical disabilities preclude such a visit. The last time I was in East London with Silversea Cruises, there was no city tour offered. The ship's shuttle bus service was to a suburban shopping mall. Thus unless one booked a tour to a game reserve, there was nothing for guests to do, and this is quite typical of what other cruise lines provide in East London.

THE CENTER OF EAST LONDON

Central East London

This map is best viewed directly from OpenStreetMap.com on your personal device where it can be expanded or one specific area can be enlarged. Given the format of this book, it is impossible to display maps with the level of detail you might wish to have while actually out exploring the city. But the OpenStreetMap maps used directly are the tool I always rely upon.

The skyline of East London seen from the ship

The East London beachfront

The Port of East London on the Buffalo River

The East London downtown skyline, (Work of South African Tourism)

The tower of the East London City Hall

The main facade of the East London City Hall (Work of Bfluff, CC BY SA 3.0 Wikimedia.org)

Tribal goods for sale along the beach, (South African Tourism)

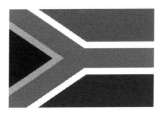

TOURING AROUND DURBAN

The greater Durban region (© OpenStreetMap contributors)

Durban is the third largest city in South Africa, but surprisingly it is not the capital of KwaZulu-Natal. The capital is located in the much smaller city of Pietermaritzberg located inland from the coast, originally founded by Dutch settlers in 1837. The metropolitan population of Durban is a substantial 3,442,000, placing it just behind Cape Town by a small margin. Black African people make up just over 50 percent of the urban population, the majority being of the great Zulu nation where once King Shaka held the British at bay in the mid 19th century. The European population of the city is far smaller than that of Cape Town, here only 15 percent of the community, but the Asian population accounts for 24 percent of Durban's population. This is the highest Asian concentration in all of South Africa, the result of the British having brought Indian workers to the plantations of KwaZulu-Natal in the mid 19th century. English is considered the primary language by almost half the population, showing the strong British colonial influence of the entire region. But 33 percent consider Zulu as their primary language at home.

All cruise ships that circumnavigate the South African coast stop in Durban for a full day, as this is the largest port on the eastern coast of the country, the main shipping center for Johannesburg and Pretoria. And for the visitor there is a lot to see and do in and around the city Durban during the one-day port call.

THE SETTING: Durban is well into the subtropical climatic zone, having nearly 1016 millimeters or 40 inches of rain per year, with over 33 percent of the days each year in which rain falls. Summers are very hot and humid, and thought not monsoonal, summer is the season for the heaviest rainfall. Winter days are generally mild and the nights actually become a bit chilly, but frost is rare and there has not been any recorded snowfall.

The countryside around Durban is one of hills and valleys that are both very green, a mix of grasses and woodland. Rivers are relatively fast flowing, as they are coming from the northwest of the province where the Drakensburg Mountains rise to the highest elevations in South Africa. They are technically not mountains, but rather the uplifted escarpment of the great interior plateau. The Drakensburg are deeply eroded with craggy peaks and impressive gorges or valleys. The highest peak is 3,482 meters or 11,424 feet above sea level, an impressive height not found anywhere else in the southern third of Africa. Given that the latitude of much of KwaZulu-Natal is subtropical, as moist air in winter flows off the Indian Ocean and rises over the ridges of the Drakensburg, snow is a common occurrence in the high mountain valleys and on the peaks. The mountain kingdom of Lesotho, which is surrounded by South Africa, is regularly blanketed with snowfall during July and August. Durban residents can spend weekends in the Drakensburg enjoying winter sports, though skiing is not a widely practiced sport because there are so few areas in which it could be practiced. But Durban residents can take advantage of enjoying a winter setting. Lesotho's mountains also attract residents from greater Johannesburg, which is still farther to the north.

DURBAN HISTORY: Prior to the arrival of the Bantu people from the north, rather primitive hunter-gatherer tribes inhabited the area as far back as 100,000 years ago. As the more advanced and aggressive Bantu people arrived, it is assumed that the earlier people either were absorbed or killed, as none of their descendants exist today.

A Portuguese ship under command of Vasco da Gama sailed along the coast in 1497 around Christmas time. He noted the landscape that was green and inviting, calling it Natal, which in means Christmas in Portuguese. But as along the rest of the coast, Portugal never encouraged settlement or laid claim to the land. Yet the Portuguese did eventually lay claim to lands to the north of South Africa on both coasts, giving rise to what are today the nations of Angola on the Atlantic coast north of Namibia and Mozambique on the Indian Ocean coast immediately adjacent to South Africa.

The Dutch in Cape Colony expanded outward, but did not attempt to extend into this area until the late 1830's. It was the British who in 1824 sent a small military group to establish a settlement along what is now the Bay of Natal, calling it Port Natal, but it eventually became known as Durban. One of the most interesting chapters in British-Zulu relationships developed as a result of this early settlement. It became the basis for a BBC mini-series many years ago called "Shaka Zulu." One member of the settlement party, a man named Henry Fynn went to the kraal of King Shaka to attempt to establish a relationship. The king had been wounded and Mr. Fynn tended his injury and enabled a speedy recovery. In gratitude King Shaka granted him a length of approximately 30 miles along the coastline, extending 100 miles inland. Mr. Fynn and the early colonists established their town within this zone, and named it in honor of the Cape Colony governor d'Urban.

The Dutch did finally establish themselves in what is now KwaZulu-Natal in 1837, creating what they called the Republic of Natalia in 1838. Their capital was at Pietermaritzburg, located about 128 kilometers or 80 miles inland from present day Durban. The area they chose was within the Zulu nation, but not well inhabited. At first relations were amicable, as one of the Voortrekkers (the name given to Dutch settlers moving inland) won concessions from the king in return for helping recover stolen livestock from a rival tribe. Despite the success, the king changed his mind and ordered all of the Voortrekkers who had settled in his territory to be slaughtered. The group that had come to the king's kraal was slaughtered, as were some outlying settlers, but the main body of those near their new capital managed to repulse the Zulu, with heavy losses on both sides.

The British in Durban sent a small contingent to help the Dutch, but they were outnumbered by the Zulu and retreated back and ultimately all of the survivors in Durban had to take refuge on board a ship, temporarily abandoning their settlement. Surprisingly the main body of Dutch Voortrekkers who had created their republic managed to hold on to their territory, but was still in danger of total extermination by the massive Zulu forces. What happened next was to set the stage for the worst battle between the Europeans and the Zulu, later to be known as the Battle of Blood River.

In December 1838, the Dutch received reinforcements under the command of Andries Pretorius for whom the national administrative capital of South Africa would ultimately be named. Pretorius looked for a site that would give his forces an advantage, as in previous skirmishes the Voortrekkers had been outmaneuvered by the Zulu. But luck was not on their side. Over 30,000 Zulu, formed into regiments, attacked with ferocity despite the Dutch having firearms and cannons. After many hours, the Zulu lost about ten percent of their army and withdrew because they saw they were no match against firepower. As they crossed the river back toward their camp, their dead had turned the river red with their blood.

While this battle was taking place, British forces took full command of Durban to prevent any Voortrekker force from laying claim to the coastal colony. It was believed that by keeping the Dutch contained in the interior adjacent to their Zulu enemy, the British would have the upper hand through control of access via the Bay of Durban, a critical move on their part. The Voortrekkers of the Republic of Natalia now tried a different strategy. The Dutch military leader Pretorius allied himself with the brother of the Zulu king after the defeat in the Battle of Blood River and a later defeat against the rival Swazi nation. The brother, named Mpande, was victorious with Dutch assistance, Pretorius was able to claim a vast tract of land for his followers, but it is not clear as to their allegiance to the Republic of Natalia.

What ultimately brought the Republic of Natalia down was its governmental structure that dictated changes in the governing council on a very frequent basis, thus destabilizing its ability to pass laws that would remain in force. They did, however, petition the British governor in the Cape Colony for recognition as an independent nation. Andries Pretorius was concerned about the Xhosa on his western border and attacked them in 1840. This prompted the British governor to put aside his sympathies for the Dutch, and he strengthened his hold on Durban. The Dutch protested, and even received naval support from the Netherlands in 1842, given written assurance of aid if the British attempted to assert their control over the new republic.

In April 1842, the British dispatched a full garrison to occupy Port Natal (Durban) and this brought strong protest from the government in Pietermaritzberg. Ultimately conflict broke out between the British and Dutch in June 1842 at the Voortrekker town of Congella just outside of Durban, resulting in Dutch losses, something the British had wanted to avoid. The final British decision was to annex the Republic of Natalia in April 1843, but to give the Dutch much latitude in local affairs. You must remember that from the time of the British takeover of the Cape Colony, all Dutch colonists became British subjects and many of those who had founded the Republic of Natalia had been born on what was British colonial soil. Those who would not acknowledge British rule found their only answer was to trek over the Drakensburg onto the Highveld and settle in the Orange Free State and Transvaal, which were beyond British jurisdiction, having been founded by the first Dutch or Boer trek out from Cape Town in the early years of the 19th century.

The new Colony of Natal became a part of the Cape Colony in 1844, and by this time only a few thousand Dutch had remained. This enabled more British colonists to begin to establish themselves in Natal, which ultimately led to the battles of the Anglo-Zulu War of 1879. In this war, the Zulu were defeated and their homeland became a part of Natal. Today Zululand is a major part of KwaZulu-Natal, its hereditary king, who is an important figure in provincial politics, still rules locally over the people. The entire province is strongly influenced by the Zulu culture, especially now that Apartheid has ended and black majority rule has been established nationwide because in KwaZulu-Natal they are the majority of the Black African population.

As British and other European settlers came to Durban, they discovered that the climate was very conducive to the raising of sugar cane on large plantations. But the raising of cane requires a lot of labor and the Zulu were not at all interested in working for white planters. Thus in the 1860's, the British began to bring cheap labor over from India and Pakistan. As the country's racial segregation policies continued to strengthen, the Asian people were classed in a category just above that of being white, a higher classification than Black African or Coloured. But none-the-less they were still segregated in all aspects of life. One Indian lawyer challenged the system and won some concessions in the early 20th century. And his name was Mohandas Gandhi. This was before he went to India where he became the father of the new nation of India in 1947.

Durban today has the largest Asian population on the African continent, the majority being of Indian or Pakistani descent, with Islam and Hindu faiths still practiced. The largest mosque in South Africa is located in the heart of downtown Durban. The Indian population of South Africa is the largest such concentration in the world outside of India. And many have become merchants, today being a strong component of Durban's upper and middle-income community.

MODERN DURBAN: The city is very dynamic, and sprawls over 2,292 square kilometers or 885 square miles. It is essentially a low-density city with the majority of residents living in single-family houses amid thick woodlands, making it the greenest city in the country. The city center has an impressive high-rise skyline, especially along the beachfront that adjoins the business district. Suburban growth has expanded into the surrounding hills, and the suburbs are connected with the city center by a good expressway system. The northern suburban area of Umhlanga is one of the newest and most rapidly developing upscale districts, and it contains numerous high-rise apartments and condominiums along its beachfront. There is one massive shopping mall in Umhlanga that is a South African showplace.

The city of Durban is the ocean playground for the millions of tourists who come from the interior urban province of Gauteng (Johannesburg and Pretoria). The Golden Mile is the designation for the downtown beachfront, which has seen a lot of redevelopment since 2009, and at its northern end is the large Moses Mabidha Stadium, built for the 2010 World Cup and the uShaka Marine World at the southern tip of the downtown beachfront. Although Cape Town is larger population wise, Durban is the second most diversified and industrialized city in the country after Johannesburg, and it accounts for 15 percent of the nation's GDP. Durban is the largest container port in South African, has diverse manufacturing and also a major financial sector along with tourism.

Since the end of Apartheid, the city has experienced problems when it has come to attempting to remove people from districts where they have been living in shacks, or what are called informal communities. There was a major attack on a group of youths in the Kennedy Road community of Durban in 2009, supposedly supported by the African National Congress and condoned by the police and later the courts. The youths were from the Abahlali Base Mjondolo movement, a group that has advocated public housing and no forced evictions for shack dwellers who are at the bottom of the economic scale. The group does not support the ANC or Democratic Alliance parties and is not well thought of by political leaders. This incident has in some ways given Durban a so-called social "black eye."

I have presented this detailed history because it is necessary to know how Durban evolved to be able to appreciate the city you will be seeing. Durban is fascinating, but you must be aware that overall, Durban does have a relatively high crime rate, especially muggings and home burglaries. For visitors, especially off of cruise ships, who are not familiar with the city it is inadvisable for you to go off on their own without engaging the services of a car and driver/guide unless going on ship sponsored tours. Even walking around the downtown area on your own is a bit dicey even though most ships offer shuttle service into the city center. If your ship shuttle is to an address along the Golden Mile, it is far safer for you to go off on your own. But every precaution not to be conspicuous with regard to dress and carrying of purses or cameras should be made to insure your safe enjoyment.

WHAT TO SEE: Just within the Durban metropolitan area there are many sights of interest. Given the size of the city and the difficulty with which a tourist on a first visit would have in getting oriented, it is best to take one of the ship's organized tours of the city so that of you do not risk going astray into some area of the city that has a higher than average crime rate. The other alternatives are:

* Having a private car and driver/guide. This can be arranged through your cruise line, but some companies do have a high markup on the actual cost. One company that specializes in offering private tours is Tours by Locals. You can check their web page at *www.toursbylocals.com/Durban-Tours.* Another widely used company is African Blue Tours and their web page is *www.africanbluetours.com/durban-tours* where you will see both city and surrounding countryside options.

* A company called Durban Taxi Service can provide tours of the city on an hourly basis. And you can contact them to see if you can arrange a tour with the taxi meeting you on the dock when the ship arrives. Check their web page at *www.eastcoastcabs.co.za* for more information.

* There is a version of the hop on hop off bus in Durban called Durban Ricksha Bus. They do offer tours of the city where you can disembark and then wait for the next bus at various stops. However, it is not the type of tour where you hop off. You can board at various locations, but you are advised to remain on board for the whole tour. Refreshments are also served onboard. There are two three-hour tours, one at 9 AM and one at 1 PM. You purchase tickets and board along the Beachfront of the Golden Mile at 1 KE Masinga Bay of Plenty, North Beach.

I have listed below the major sights within the city that I consider give you the best overall approach to coming to know this large urban area. (shown in alphabetical order):

* **Durban Art Gallery** - It has a major collection of African art and handcraft located in the City Hall on the second floor. The collection is quite interesting and especially colorful. The gallery is open Monday thru Saturday from 8 AM to 6 PM.

* **Durban Botanical Gardens** - A collection of tropical plants that represent much of Africa, with emphasis upon the local region. And the trees of the garden are filled with native

monkeys. Apart from the beautifully manicured and arranged floral exhibits, you almost are able to believe you are not in the city, but out in the wilds of the forests of KwaZulu-Natal. This is a popular spot where bridal parties come for photos. If you wish to photograph a bridal party, just ask and they will most likely oblige. But be sure to wish them happiness. The garden is open daily from 7:30 AM to 6:15 PM. It is very close in to the downtown core.

* Durban City Hall and Natural Science Museum - The city hall is a fine example of very ornate Roman style Victorian Era public architecture. The building is quite grand and it is patterned after the city hall in Belfast, Northern Ireland. The natural science museum is inside the city hall building, and a good interactive venue for the enjoyment of the natural science of the world with emphasis upon South Africa. The museum is open Monday thru Saturday from 9 AM to 4 PM and Sunday from 11 AM to 4 PM.

* Florida Road - In the suburb of Windermere, this is a very upscale shopping and restaurant district that also has excellent Victorian architecture. There is a strong similarity in architectural flavor and also the richness of the trees and flowers to suburbs you would see in Sydney, Australia. There are also many outdoor cafes where you can enjoy a light refreshment or lunch.

* Gateway Theatre of Shopping - This is a dynamic and massive shopping center, said to be the largest shopping mall on the African continent. It is located in the northern beach suburb of Umhlanga and is quite a showpiece. The architectural design and size of the mall make it worthy of a visit even if you are not into shopping. The mall is open from 9 AM to 7 PM Monday thru Thursday and from 9 AM to 7PM, Friday and Saturday from 9 AM to 9 PM and Sunday from 9 AM to 6 PM.

* Golden Mile - The core of the tourist focus is this high-rise lined beach strip adjacent to the city center. The beaches and parks make this a prime venue and are safe for visitors from the ship to walk during the day. Many cruise line shuttle busses bring guests to the Golden Mile. And local artisans and craftsmen have their wares displayed and for sale along the main promenade.

* Indian Quarter - A section of downtown Durban in which the shops and public buildings are the core of the Indian community. It is enjoyable to walk through this district and sample the sights and aromas. You can also stop in and visit the largest Islamic mosque in South Africa. But you should be in the company of your guide, as it is not totally safe for foreign visitors to be walking alone.

* Jonnson Kings Park Stadium - The home stadium for the Durban Sharks, a well-renowned rugby team. There is a gift shop within the stadium selling Sharks memorabilia. No guided tours are posted as being offered.

* Jumah Mosque - Located in the Indian Quarter, this is the largest mosque in the Southern Hemisphere, and its architecture is a mix of Islamic and British Victorian styles. This is a Sunni mosque and can hold over 6,000 worshipers at one time. You are advised to have a guide with you when visiting the mosque. And it is customary to remove your shoes at the

entrance. No specific hours are posted. I do caution you not to visit on Friday, as this is the sabbath day in Islam.

* Kwa Muhle Museum - A very important museum that chronicles the history of Apartheid, and it is an emotional experience, as it was practiced in KwaZulu-Natal. It is a very illuminating experience, almost as dramatic as the Apartheid Museum in Johannesburg. The museum is open Monday thru Friday from 8:30 AM to 4 PM and closes at 12:30 PM on Saturday. It is located at 130 Bram Fischer Road in central Durban.

* Markets of Warwick - This is a very exciting and large outdoor street markets where all the peoples of Durban mingle. It is located in Warwick Junction on the edge of the downtown. Tours of the markets are offered. Check with the market via email at *mowtours@ac.org.za* for booking information.

* Moses Mabhida Stadium - This 2010 stadium built for the World Cup is the pride of the city. There is a bungee jumping program from the highest part of the stadium, which is fascinating to watch unless you feel like participating. There is also a dramatic sky view platform where you can see all of Durban. Check the web page for details as to the various tours available at *www.mmstadium.com*.

* Suncoast Casino and Entertainment World - A massive casino and entertainment complex at the north end of the Golden Mile, this is a very popular venue for Durban residents and visitors alike. The casino complex is quite large and offers dining facilities, hotel accommodation, shopping and gaming. It is open 24-hours seven days a week.

* Umhlanga - The newest upscale suburban district along the beachfront north of the city. Here you will find several posh hotels, restaurants and Durban's massive and fashionable Gateway Theatre of Shopping. Umhlanga is the most fashionable hotel and beach district of Durban and is rapidly becoming a major South African attraction.

* uShaka Marine World - A spectacular water park and aquarium at the south end of the Golden Mile. This is a 15 hectare or 37 acre theme park that contains its own beach, tribal village, marine aquarium and outdoor maritime exhibits. Many ship shuttles will bring guests here as the drop off point. The park is open daily from 9 AM to 5 PM and is a major Durban attraction.

TOURS OUTSIDE OF DURBAN: Outside of the city there are some very important venues that may be included on all day tours or that you can visit on your own with a car and driver/guide or your cruise line may possibly offer a tour. These venues are:

* PheZulu Safari Park - This venue located a short distance outside of the city to the west gives you a chance to understand Zulu culture by visiting the traditionally built village. Beyond the village is a snake and crocodile farm, but you will not be in a true game park where you would have a chance to see African wildlife, as the Durban area is too heavily populated and the hinterland too well developed with small villages and farms. The village

puts on a show for visitors and it does give you a feeling for traditional Zulu culture. The park is open daily from 8 AM to 4:30 PM and is quite enjoyable.

* Umgeni River Bird Park - The Park is located under high cliffs alongside the Umgeni River just on the northern outskirts of Durban. There are beautiful outdoor walks as well as aviaries to visit where you will see tropical birds representing Africa and other continents> The array of birds and the setting combine to give you a true tropical experience. The park is open from 9 AM to 5 PM daily. The drive there and back is short so this is not a long trip and you can still have time to explore the city.

* Valley of a Thousand Hills - To visit this region, you will spend most of your day and miss the city proper. This is a part of Zululand and you will see both stunning scenery, Zulu villages and experience some of the culture of the Zulu people. You will also learn about the life and role of King Shaka and how the region was once a great battleground between the Zulu, the Dutch and British. King Shaka was so important to the history of the region that even Durban's international airport is named King Shaka International.

FINAL WORDS: Once again I recommend either a ship sponsored tour or that you hire a private car and driver/guide. Durban is simply too large a city in which to try and get about on your own. And as is true in all large South African cities, there is always the possibility of becoming a victim of street crime if you look lost and are not confident about where you are going. It is an unfortunate fact of life in South Africa, but this should not deter you from having a good day in Durban. If you absolutely want to be on your own, it is safe to walk along the Golden Mile. Walking through the downtown area, the Indian Quarter and along the Golden Mile without the need of a guide is essentially alright so long as you take normal precautions with valuables and are not ostentatious.

DINING OUT: As a large city, Durban has a great array of restaurants in all price categories and representing a multiplicity of ethnic tastes. For your selection, I have chosen a grouping of top restaurants representing fine seafood, traditional South African flavors and a taste of India and Pakistan given the city's large South Asian community. The list is in alphabetical order and does not include many restaurants located in the outer suburbs except for Umhlanga, which is such a popular and up coming district. My listing is not as lengthy as you would expect for such a large city because I have found that a very large percentage of the restaurants in Durban have inconsistent quality and the local reviews for so many range from great to terrible for individual restaurants. My choices are selected from the very cream of Durban and include:

* Butcher Boys Florida Road – This restaurant is both a seafood and meat lover's paradise. It is located at 150 Florida Road in one of the most popular districts of Durban. If you love grilled steak, this is one of Durban's finest. And with regard to fresh seafood, they also grill the local catch of the day. The cuisine and service are especially good. They are open Monday thru Thursday from Noon to 10 PM, Friday and Saturday from Noon to 10:30 PM and on Sunday from Noon to 9:30 PM.

* Elements Café – In the Beverly Hills Hotel at Umhlanga Rocks, this is an outstanding restaurant overlooking the beach. The atmosphere is what must be called understated elegance mixed with modern aspects of décor. On Sunday they feature a very good brunch and you can eat out on the terrace if the weather is conducive. Their regular menu is very diverse and offers a wide array of salads, sandwiches, curries, grilled meats and poultry along with sumptuous desserts. Reservations for lunch are advised. They are open daily from Noon to 9 PM.

* Fat Fish – This is a very popular seafood restaurant located at 7 Westville Road in Westville Junction, which is quite some distance outside of the city center. Even though I have concentrated on restaurants closer in, this is in my opinion the best place in Durban for good seafood. So many of the closer in restaurants receive mixed reviews. Fat Fish is consistently good and they offer the freshest catch in both fish and shellfish. The cuisine and atmosphere are very pleasant and the service is good. They are open Monday thru Saturday from 9 AM to 8 PM and on Sunday they open at 9 AM and close at 7 PM.

* Goundens – This a very popular Indian restaurant located south of the city center in Congella at 520 Umbilo Road. The menu features both Indian and other East Asian cuisine, both vegetarian and non-vegetarian dishes being prepared. Many locals say that their curries are the best in Durban. They are open Monday thru Friday from 9 AM to 6 PM and Saturday from 9 AM to 4:30 PM.

* Habesha Café – This is a traditional African restaurant where you will be treated to the flavors of Ethiopia, a popular continental cuisine among Durban residents. They are located at 124 Helen Joseph Avenue in suburban Glenwood. The flavors of Ethiopia are very aromatic yet not overpowering as Indian curry can sometimes be. Ethiopian cuisine has been spread all through modern eastern and southern Africa, as a popular favorite. This restaurant is open Monday thru Saturday from 8 AM to 10 PM.

* Havana Grill – Located in the Suncoast Casino, this restaurant despite its name is not Cuban. The diverse menu is very international and they do feature vegetarian dishes as well as an array of meats, poultry and seafood. They have a huge array of starters and salads, followed by choices of fresh local seafood and beef. They also offer poultry dishes, pork and lamb choices as well as ostrich and venison. They follow through with excellent desserts. The cuisine, service and atmosphere are all outstanding. They are open Monday thru Saturday from Noon to 10 PM and on Sunday from Noon to 5 PM and again from 6 to 8 PM.

* Little India Restaurant – At 155 Musgrave Road in suburban Musgrave, this is one of the most popular Indian restaurants in Durban. They feature a wide array of traditional dishes both vegetarian and non-vegetarian, but all prepared to perfection. Their hours are from 11 AM to 10 PM daily and you will not be disappointed.

* Mali's Indian Restaurant – Located in Morningside just north of the city center at 77 Smiso Nkwanyana Road, this is a very well respected Indian restaurant offering a true taste of the spicy cuisine in which curry is a major factor. The dishes are all beautifully prepared and expertly presented in a very comfortable atmosphere. Many of the dishes represent the

vegetarian tastes so dominant in Indian culture, but there are meat and poultry offerings as well. Lunch is served Tuesday thru Sunday from 12:30 to 3:30 PM and dinner is served Tuesday thru Saturday from 5:30 to 10 PM and on Sunday from 5:30 to 9 PM.

* Olive and Oil – This casual restaurant features seafood served Mediterranean style and also excellent pizza. They are located at 149 Bulwer Road just west of the city center. They are open from Noon to 3 PM daily for lunch, Sunday and Monday from 6 to 9 PM for dinner and Tuesday thru Saturday from 6 to 10 PM for dinner.

* Parc – This is a popular restaurant located at 394 Esther Roberts Road, 2-A Oslo Building in Glenwood. Their menu is a fusion of many tastes and they pride themselves in offering healthy menu choices using fresh ingredients. And their menu changes with the seasons, offering what is freshest at the time. They serve breakfast and lunch Tuesday thru Friday from 7:30 AM to 4 PM and on Saturday and Sunday from 8 AM to 2 PM.

FINAL WORDS: Durban is a very distinctive city given its lush tropical setting. Cape Town has a Mediterranean climate, which is overall moderately dry. Johannesburg is located on the High Veld and has a subtropical savannah climate, which is also moderately dry. But Durban is lush and green in its tropical setting. The flavor of the city mixes British, Dutch and South Indian cultures together with its Zulu majority. All of these distinctions make Durban a fascinating city that is most unique.

As a large city it is best to either use a ship sponsored tour or have a private car and driver/guide to be able to explore the many facets of this fascinating city. But given the relatively high crime rate, it is not a place to go exploring on your own.

DURBAN MAPS

THE CENTRAL CITY OF DURBAN

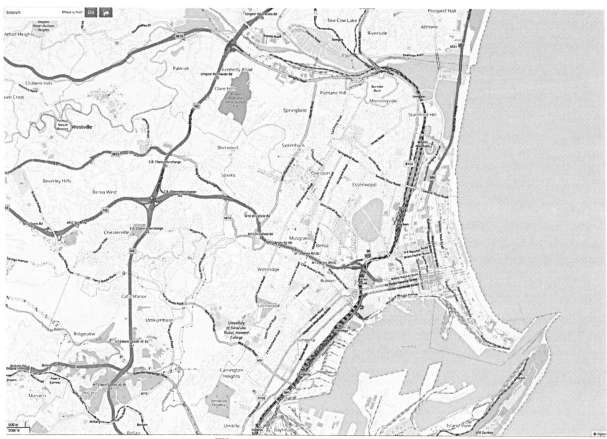

The central area of Durban

This map is best viewed directly from OpenStreetMap.com on your personal device where it can be expanded or one specific area can be enlarged. Given the format of this book, it is impossible to display maps with the level of detail you might wish to have while actually out exploring the city. But the OpenStreetMap maps used directly are the tool I always rely upon.

THE CENTRAL CORE OF DURBAN

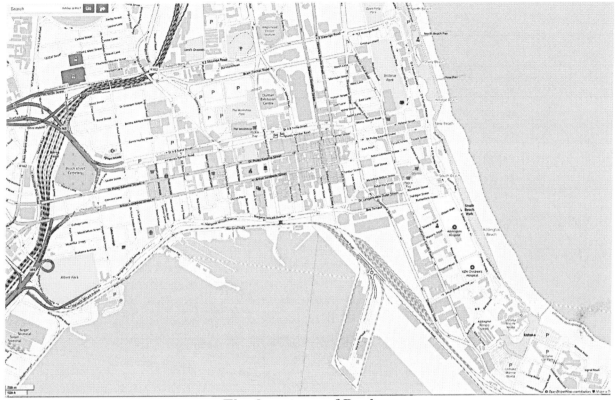

The downtown of Durban

This map is best viewed directly from OpenStreetMap.com on your personal device where it can be expanded or one specific area can be enlarged. Given the format of this book, it is impossible to display maps with the level of detail you might wish to have while actually out exploring the city. But the OpenStreetMap maps used directly are the tool I always rely upon.

THE BOTANICAL GARDEN AREA OF DURBAN

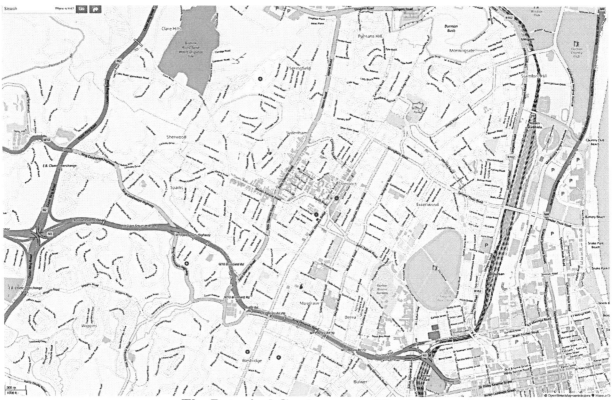

The Botanical Garden area of Durban

This map is best viewed directly from OpenStreetMap.com on your personal device where it can be expanded or one specific area can be enlarged. Given the format of this book, it is impossible to display maps with the level of detail you might wish to have while actually out exploring the city. But the OpenStreetMap maps used directly are the tool I always rely upon.

THE UMHLANGA BEACH AREA OF DURBAN

The beach suburb of Umhlanga

This map is best viewed directly from OpenStreetMap.com on your personal device where it can be expanded or one specific area can be enlarged. Given the format of this book, it is impossible to display maps with the level of detail you might wish to have while actually out exploring the city. But the OpenStreetMap maps used directly are the tool I always rely upon.

An aerial view looking into the heart of Durban (Work of Andres de Wet, CC BY SA 3.0, Wikimedia.org)

An aerial view of downtown Durban, (Work of Esther Dyson, CC BY SA 2.0, Wikimedia.org)

Along the Esplanade on the Golden Mile

Vendors selling their wares on the Golden Mile

The recreational amenities on the beach of the Golden Mile

West Street in the heart of downtown Durban at Christmas time

Another view on West Street in downtown Durban reflecting Victorian architecture

The Victorian architecture of Durban City Hall

The great mosque in the Indian quarter of downtown Durban

Moses Mabhida Stadium

Suncoast Casino at the top end of the Golden Mile

Victorian architecture along Florida Street in Windemere

A mix of housing styles in suburban Morningside

In the Durban Botanical Garden

The beach at Umhlanga Rocks from the Beverly Hills Hotel

Inside the massive Gateway Theatre of Shopping in Umhlanga

The lush green outer suburbs of Durban

In the Valley of a Thousand Hills (Work of Jean & Nathalie, CC BY SA 2.0, Wikimedia.org)

In the Umgeni River Bird Park, (Work of Sherwin, CC BY SA $.0, Wikimedia.org)

VISITING REMOTE RICHARDS BAY

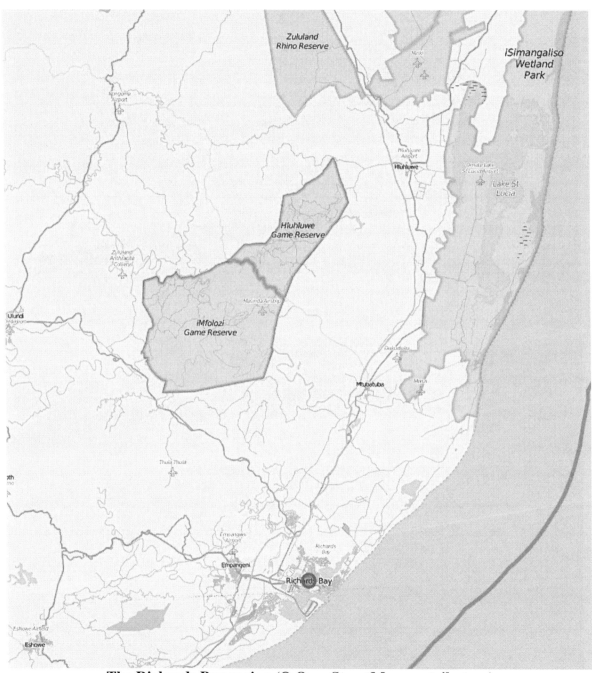

The Richards Bay region (© OpenStreetMap contributors)

Richards Bay is included in almost all South African cruise itineraries, but not because of the attractions offered by the town. It is rather for the opportunity to visit regional game parks or Zulu cultural centers that most itineraries include Richards Bay and many are based upon an overnight stay to allow guests to have two full days of sightseeing. There is no actual city of Richards Bay in the physical sense. Yes it is an incorporated municipality, but rather than being a single city, it is a collection of residential communities housing port and industrial workers. This is a major industrial zone because of its massive sheltered harbor and its proximity to the Johannesburg-Pretoria region. The total population of all the small communities that comprise Richards Bay is 57,000, but no one area is more significant than any other. And there is no central business or civic core that speaks to this being a city. The population composition is just over 40 percent Black African, 18 percent Asian and a significant 30 percent European. Zulu is the primary language for the African population while English is the language used by most Asian and European families. Afrikaans is spoken on a daily basis by just over 20 percent of the local population.

Richards Bay is located in the far northeastern portion of KwaZulu-Natal, an area that is still predominantly wild country where game reserves are an important element of the landscape. Because this is not a well-settled region, there is the problem of malaria, and you should be advised that most South African doctors recommend a course of anti-malarial medication that usually commences one to two days prior to your visit and continues for one to two days following. There is no preventative vaccine for malaria. Chances of being bitten by a mosquito are slim during daylight hours unless you are trekking through swampy areas, which the various tours do not include. And if you are simply visiting the Zulu cultural centers as your primary tour or staying in Richards Bay, there would be no need for taking the preventative medication because for many people it does have significant side effects.

THE SETTING: The countryside of northeastern South Africa is still classified as being subtropical, as the Tropic of Capricorn is a few degrees of latitude farther north. But it is a very warm and humid subtropical region, average rainfall being slightly above 1,220 millimeters or 48 inches. Most of the rainfall comes during the summer monsoonal period, but winters are also humid with significant rainfall. Temperatures during the summer months can reach into the mid 30's Celsius or 90's Fahrenheit and humidity combined with temperature give it a tropical feeling.

The land is essentially a flat coastal plain with sandy soil. There are some coastal dunes and tidal inlets with swampy margins. Inland to the west and northwest, the land begins to rise into low hills. The outer mountain-like edge of the great interior plateau is now well away from this lowland region. Vegetation cover consists of a mix of scrub woodland with pockets of mixed tropical forest growth. The area never receives frost or snow, thus presenting a consistently green appearance.

HISTORY: Richards Bay does not have a long or complex history. The first note comes during the Anglo-Zulu War of 1879 when the British Commodore for the Cape Region established a small harbor to give additional access to the interior for troops and supplies.

The town only dates to 1954 when the first harbor facilities were established. The major deep-water harbor was the result of government action to provide greater access to Johannesburg and the interior. To create a viable harbor required the building of a railway line and the creation of oil and gas pipelines between Richards Bay and Johannesburg. The harbor was opened in 1976 after four years of intensive construction. When the residential communities were first established in the 1970's, they were exclusively for white Europeans only. The Black African workers were housed 16 kilometers or 10 miles away from the harbor facilities in a designated township called Esikhaweni. The suburb of Veld-en-Vlei was created in the mid 1980's, but only for Asian and Colored peoples. This of course was typical of the Apartheid Era. Today there is no official segregation based upon skin color or national origin. The only requirements to live in what were once white only suburbs is to be able to afford the price of the real estate, something still very difficult for most non-whites to do. Thus in essence the old segregated system is still unofficially in effect, but now it is economic segregation.

The area has attracted a lot of industrial development, and this is why Richards Bay is not a tourist destination in and of itself. There is a coal exporting port that is the world's largest. There are two aluminum smelters because of the available power. Local mining of iron ore adds to the mineral export role. Rare zircon and granite are also mined in the area. There are numerous other industrial and manufacturing plants located around the harbor facility producing a variety of chemical and wood products. Despite the amount of industry, there is a high rate of unemployment and moderate crime in the region. The unemployment is the result of the world's recession of 2008 combined with a post-recession movement of people from rural areas to Richards Bay expecting to find work.

WHAT TO SEE: Tourism is an important part of the local economy, but not for the amenities of Richards Bay. The region is home to many game reserves, national parks and Zulu cultural centers. And this is why your cruise ship will call at Richards Bay. Some cruise lines offer a shuttle bus to the major shopping mall for those who do not wish to take a tour. Frankly this is a total waste of time because the mall is catering to a blue-collar populace and it does not have any major anchor stores and limited shops selling souvenir or craft items. The dock area is adjacent to a small marina and local Zulu artisans come and set up a local craft market, but once again this would not be capable of occupying you for an entire day.

* Some cruise lines may be able to provide a private car and driver/guide, but the availability is limited so it will be on a first come basis. There is one limousine service provider that may be willing to offer private touring. Richards Bay Harbour Limousine Hire has a web page at *www.booksouthafrica.travel/listingsrichards-bay-limousine-hire.* There are several self-drive services available, but I would caution against driving on your own. Remember that in South Africa traffic moves on the left. Also the roads in this region are rather limited and it would be quite easy to get lost, and safety in rural areas cannot be guaranteed.

* There is local taxi service but the possibility of arranging anything other than local touring in and around the community is doubtful. You can check out Richards Bay Taxi Service at *www.booksouthafrica.travel/listings/richards-bay-taxi-services* for further details.

* There obviously is no hop on hop off bus or trolley service in Richards Bay, as there is nothing to see within the town area.

Here are my recommendations for things to do, most of them no doubt included in the cruise excursion itinerary:

   * **Damazulu Traditional Village** - This is the newest cultural venue that was officially opened by the Zulu King. Although visitors are an important factor, this is a traditional village where several families are still maintaining the Zulu lifestyle that would have been seen by colonials. The village is close to Richards Bay. There are three special shows per day, so it is important to book ahead if you are going with your own car and driver/guide. The web page is www.sa-venues.com where you can find more detail. Shows are performed at 8:15 AM, 11 AM including a lunch and 3:15 PM.

* **Hluhluwe-Umfolozi Game Reserve** - This is a magnificent reserve, covering a mix of savanna and woodland spread over more than 200,000 acres. Here is where you will have a chance to see the big 5 animals that are so sought after by people coming to South Africa. The big 5 include lions, leopards, rhinos (especially the rare white rhino), elephants and water buffalo. There is never any guarantee you will see all five, but this park is one of the best for wildlife viewing. The park also includes many wetlands where you have a chance to see hippos enjoying the water, crocodiles and many species of aquatic birds. This reserve is the main focus of ship sponsored tours. It would be very difficult, if not impossible, to arrange a visit on your own with a car and driver/guide, as they are generally well booked with group tours.

* **Outdoor Africa** - This is a company that will take small groups or individuals out to view local wildlife. The advantage is that you can customize what it is you want to see and how long you wish to be out. Your ship's shore excursion office should be able to make private arrangements with this well respected company. You would need to contact them via their web page at www.outdoor-africa.com to arrange for a private tour providing you have already arranged transportation there and back.

* **Richards Bay Game Reserve** - A smaller reserve where you will not find the big 5. But you will see hippos, crocodiles, wading birds and many species of monkeys in the trees. This reserve is very close to Richards Bay and can be seen on a shorter visit, especially good for those who tire too easily on a long full day excursion. Your cruise line may offer a half-day visit. If you have arranged for a private car and driver/guide, this is a good venue that is close to the port. Check their web page at www.sa-venues.com and then search Richards Bay.

* **Shakaland** - This is the best-known Zulu cultural center, and much of it was built as the set for the famous BBC mini-series "Shaka Zulu." There is also an onsite hotel, dining room and conference center. It is quite tourist oriented, yet still essentially the experience is authentic and cruise passengers with limited mobility find it most appealing since it is an easy activity.

Richards Bay is well known for its beautiful coastal beaches where simply sunbathing or more active surfing are available. For those who wish to dive, the St Lucia Marine Reserve north of the town has facilities. But again you will need transportation to either the beach or the reserve where diving is possible.

DINING OUT: Cruise ships dock adjacent to the local marina. There are café facilities within walking distance of the ship. But to find a good restaurant there are a few choices around the Boardwalk Mall where most shuttle busses drop ship passengers or right at the marina adjacent to the cruise ship dock. But the majority are rather poor in quality or inconsistent. Because of the lack of standards that I hold in recommending restaurants, here are my two choices shown alphabetically:

* KNK Curries – Located in the small marina adjacent to where the cruise ships dock, this restaurant is only mere steps from the ship. It is a traditional East Indian restaurant featuring a variety of curries and dishes to satisfy vegetarian and vegan tastes. The restaurant is open Monday thru Thursday from 8 AM to 6 PM, Friday thru Sunday from 8 AM to 7 PM.

* Panarotis Boardwalk Express – Located in the Boardwalk Mall, Shop number 32a, this restaurant features Italian pasta dishes and a variety of pizzas. And the restaurant also offers vegetarian fare as well. The dishes are well prepared and the service is good. This is more of a family type restaurant, but Richards Bay does not have a great variety of dining experiences. They are open Sunday thru Friday from 9 AM to 10 PM and Saturday from 9 AM to 11 PM.

FINAL WORDS: As you can see from the fact that there are no sightseeing possibilities worthy of note in Richards Bay and only two restaurants that barely meet my standards, this is not the type of port in which you want to spend time. Therefore, it is imperative that you plan to take some form of excursion for the day in port. Without a planned excursion, this can prove to be a rather wasted day.

RICHARDS BAY MAPS

THE URBAN AREA OF RICHARDS BAY

The harbor and the town of Richards Bay

This map is best viewed directly from OpenStreetMap.com on your personal device where it can be expanded or one specific area can be enlarged. Given the format of this book, it is impossible to display maps with the level of detail you might wish to have while actually out exploring the city. But the OpenStreetMap maps used directly are the tool I always rely upon.

THE MARINA DISTRICT

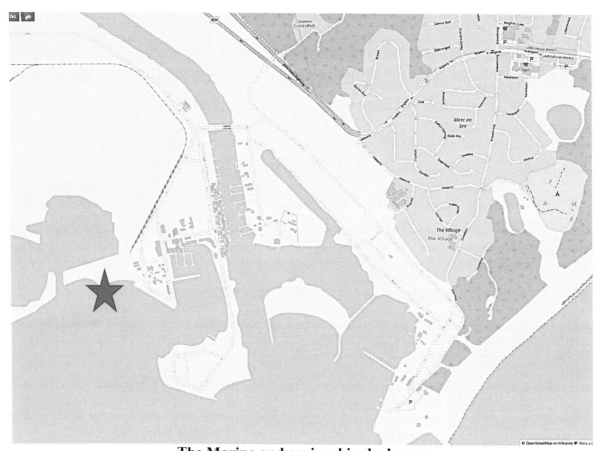

The Marina and cruise ship dock area

This map is best viewed directly from OpenStreetMap.com on your personal device where it can be expanded or one specific area can be enlarged. Given the format of this book, it is impossible to display maps with the level of detail you might wish to have while actually out exploring the city. But the OpenStreetMap maps used directly are the tool I always rely upon.

THE BOARDWALK MALL AREA

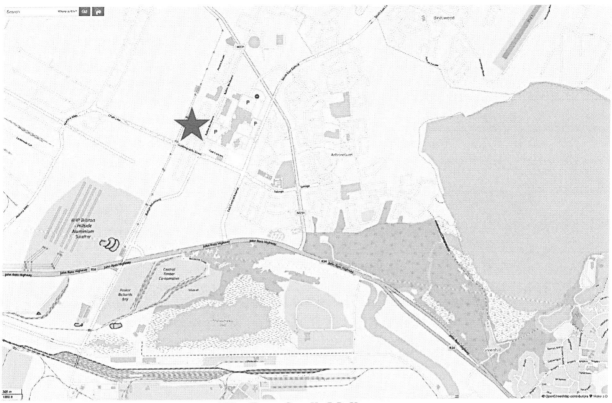

The Boardwalk Mall area

This map is best viewed directly from OpenStreetMap.com on your personal device where it can be expanded or one specific area can be enlarged. Given the format of this book, it is impossible to display maps with the level of detail you might wish to have while actually out exploring the city. But the OpenStreetMap maps used directly are the tool I always rely upon.

The Richards Bay Marina where cruise ships dock

The Richards Bay Marina with its boardwalk and shops

The Richards Bay Boardwalk (Bellingham Park) Mall

Richards Bay coal loading terminal

Rhinos at the Hluhluwe-Umfolozi Game Reserve (Work of Bagbel at wikivoyages shared)

Visiting Shakaland (Work of Georgio at fr. wikipedia)

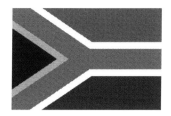

TRAVELING THROUGH GREATER JOHANNESBURG

Map of Greater Johannesburg excluding Pretoria (© OpenStreetMap contributors)

Johannesburg is the largest and most important city in South Africa. But tourists have been given a lot of misinformation regarding this very dynamic city. Yes it is true that there is a high degree of urban crime in the greater Johannesburg area. But no it is NOT true that if you go there as a visitor you are sure to be accosted and robbed, or worse even killed. The media, especially many travel sources, have maligned the city, giving the illusion that nobody should go to Johannesburg unless they have to. When I first went there, I had the vision in mind that I would not be safe even in my hotel room. At first I was fearful, but soon came to realize that with normal precautions that you would take in any major foreign metropolis, Johannesburg is a city to be enjoyed. Subsequently I have come to know the city and find it to be a fascinating, and in many ways beautiful city. There are definitely parts of the city where a visitor should not go on their own. But with a good guide who knows the city well, there are virtually no areas off limits, especially if you want to see all aspects of life in this megacity. I have been to the most crime ridden parts of the city, but properly escorted by a guide of Zulu tribal origin and was able to absorb its flavor, color and problems in total safety.

The city of Johannesburg is the central hub of the Province of Gauteng. This province also includes the satellite suburbs that surround Johannesburg, but that are not a part of the municipality. This includes the massive former township of Soweto and the national administrative capital of Pretoria (which will be treated separately). All of Gauteng, also considered as Greater Johannesburg, has a 2018 estimated population of 14,717,000 residents, including Pretoria. The immediate metropolitan population of Johannesburg is 7,860,000, including Soweto. But this does not include the 1,763,000 that make up greater Pretoria. There appears to be an attempt to amalgamate the entire province into one megalopolis in theory, yet the individual cities still administer their own affairs. In any event, Johannesburg is a large and complex metropolis, today being the third largest city on the African continent after Cairo and Lagos. It is the financial, industrial, commercial and cultural heart of the nation. And Pretoria is the administrative capital city of the nation even though Parliament meets in Cape Town and the Supreme Court holds sessions in Bloemfontein.

The majority of visitors who come to South Africa for a cruise around its coast will most often fly into Cape Town. Those who are coming by ship from Europe, making the cruise around the coast a part of a greater African cruise will generally disembark in Cape Town. Unless including a visit to Kruger National Park or one of the other interior game preserves, Johannesburg is not given consideration in the itinerary. Many travel agents will actually dissuade their clients from visiting, saying that it is too dangerous or that there is nothing worth seeing. At this point I must state this is a big mistake and a disservice to a fascinating city. Johannesburg is definitely worthy of a visit. Depending upon your itinerary and choice of flights, you can visit Johannesburg before or after your cruise. Unlike Cape Town, Johannesburg is the aviation gateway to all of southern Africa. Its international airport connects the southern part of the continent with Europe, North and South America, Australia and Asia. Cape Town has limited flight connections with Europe. I have spoken to so many cruise ship guests who have told me they did nothing more than change planes en route to or from Cape Town and had no desire to spend any time in Johannesburg.

THE BLUE TRAIN: One of the most elegant ways in which to travel between Gauteng (the greater region of Johannesburg) and Cape Town is to take the Blue Train, which begins or ends its journey in Pretoria, which is only an hour or less by motorway from the northern suburbs of Johannesburg where the best hotels are located. And the hotels will provide transportation to or from the railway station. The reason Pretoria marks the inland starting or terminating station for the Blue Train is because it is the administrative capital city for South Africa while Cape Town is the legislative capital city. South Africa is the only nation in the world with three official capitals, Bloemfontein being the judicial capital. All foreign embassies and legations are located in Pretoria where the President of South Africa resides and works.

The Blue Train is the most elegant train in the world, and the all day journey, including overnight, is exceptionally memorable. And I might add that it is also exceptionally expensive, averaging $2,800 U.S. per couple or $2,300 single for full luxury service. This may appear to be an excessive fare, but it includes a level of service and quality gourmet meals that would rival the finest world-class hotel. And the accommodations on board are not typical of most sleeping accommodations on regular trains. Here there are "real" beds and there are bathtubs, something not found on other passenger trains. The journey includes brunch, high tea, formal dinner and breakfast the following morning.

THE SETTING FOR JOHANNESBURG: Johannesburg is a city of the High Veld, the great interior grassland plateau of South Africa. The elevation is 1,753 meters or 5,751 feet above sea level, slightly more than the American city of Denver, which calls itself the "Mile High City." Because of its high elevation, Johannesburg has a mild subtropical climate. The city receives over 533 millimeters or 21 inches of rain in an average year, mostly during the summer months, as warm, moist air rises over the Drakensberg and creates afternoon and evening thundershowers across the eastern High Veld. During winter, cold fronts come across from the west, but still draw moisture off the Indian Ocean. Temperatures are relatively mild during the summer with daytime highs in the upper 20's Celsius or 80's Fahrenheit and occasionally into the mid 30's Celsius or 90's Fahrenheit, but evening cool of comfortably. During winter, daytime highs can be as low as the upper teens Celsius or 50's with occasional nighttime frost. Snow occurs once every few years and sometimes can accumulate to five to eight centimeters or two or three inches.

The High Veld around Johannesburg is a gently rolling grassland dotted with acacias and other trees, sometimes growing in small clusters. On the higher hills or low mountain ranges there are small patches of forest. The city is actually built along the outcropped rib known as the Witwatersrand. It was here that underground deposits of gold were discovered, and it was this valuable mineral that made the city grow into the nation's most important urban center. The center of the city is built north of the Witwatersrand and stretches over gently rolling terrain that drops in elevation both north and south of the main gold bearing ridge. There are no major rivers flowing through Johannesburg. And this fact makes it today the largest city in the world that has not developed along a river, on the shores of a lake or the ocean. The Witwatersrand is the watershed boundary between the great Limpopo River to the north and the Vaal River to the south, and small tributary streams feed both from greater Johannesburg. Historically the Vaal was the southern border of the former province known as Transvaal where the Boers settled well beyond British control. The Vaal is a tributary to the Orange River, thus Johannesburg contributes to two of southern Africa's major river systems. The very name Transvaal represented the fact that when the Boers trekked north they crossed the Vaal before settling, thus trans-Vaal meant north of the river.

SETTLEMENT HISTORY: The San people initially inhabited The High Veld when Bantu tribes began to migrate south and slowly take over the land starting in the 13th century of our calendar. By the 1700's, the Bantu-speaking Sotho-Twana people dominated the region of what is now Johannesburg. And today they are the tribe that comprises the small nation of Lesotho on the edge of the Drakensberg. They were and still are highly advanced by pre European standards, having been agricultural and also having a knowledge of metallurgy. But by the 19th century, as the Dutch and British settlers spread along the coast into KwaZulu-Natal, the Zulu became displaced from many of their lands, and they in turn spread northward and engaged in war with the Sotho-Twana and the Swazi peoples.

The Dutch Voortrekkers began their push into the High Veld in the early 1800's, crossing the Vaal River and establishing small settlements in what would become the Transvaal Republic. Their desire to escape from the British Empire and build their own society once again was short lived. In 1881, a small gold strike was made west of present day Johannesburg in what is now known as the Cradle of Humankind. Digging in this hilly area ultimately led to finding the earliest remains of Homo sapiens, our own species. Today that area is a national park and UNESCO World Heritage Site because of its scientific importance. In 1884, gold was discovered along the Witwatersrand and word quickly spread, and the area that is now the Cradle of Humankind was forsaken by the prospectors.

Overnight the area began to grow as a typical mining camp similar to what happened in California and in the Australian colony of Victoria. By 1886, Ferreira's Camp was a typical and somewhat unkempt mining community, but it was replaced in late 1886 by a town laid out and surveyed by the government just to the north of the Witwatersrand Reef, and it was named Johannesburg. Several strikes were made in the area around Johannesburg, and soon the British became very interested in both buying the first refined gold bars and also in further exploration and exploitation. By 1896, over 100,000 people lived in Johannesburg, and it continued to grow quite rapidly in a rather helter skelter manner. Initially it was a melting pot of white miners; black mine workers, trades people, gamblers and ladies of the evening among other sorts. Tensions over land and mineral rights between the British and the Boers ultimately led to the second Boer War, bringing British occupation of Johannesburg and the entire Transvaal. During the war, most of the black labor force deserted the city, which resulted in later recruitment of Chinese workers, but they were quickly replaced when the war was over and black miners returned to the city.

The early 20th century saw Johannesburg continue to grow both outward and upward, developing the first urban skyline in South Africa. With Apartheid in 1948, many sections of the city were forcibly cleared, as blacks were forced to live in designated townships, Soweto becoming the largest, and in many ways the most dilapidated. By the 1980's, the inner city had become relegated to poor whites and colored, and the retail role moved outward to suburbs like Rosebank and Sandton where they remain today, as the most viable and upmarket shopping and dining areas in Johannesburg. The inner city became unpopular among whites because of its increasing crime rate. Since the end of Apartheid, the Hillbrow, area just north of downtown has become a high-density black residential and commercial community, and unfortunately a high crime area. Hillbrow was once primarily a white middle class community. Today it has a distinct cultural flavor, but is only safe for visitors to enter in the company of an experienced guide. The old downtown core has seen some revitalization, as many office complexes still exist in the city center and their labor force does dine at lunchtime or shop in the remaining stores. But downtown is akin to many of the large American cities where the upper and middle class white population abandons it after normal working hours.

THE VISUAL LANDSCAPE: Greater Johannesburg is a sprawling urban area with multiple nodes of importance. It is surrounded by both upmarket formerly all-white suburbs and what were once classed as townships, most of which have a mix of shantytown districts along with middle-income tract housing.

The largest former township is Soweto, located southwest of the city center, the name being a contraction of the designation as the Southwest Township. It is connected by commuter rail service. Soweto is in effect a separate city with 1,271,000 residents. It is divided into distinct neighborhoods that vary in residential quality from the poorest shanties to very nice upper middle-income districts. The majority of the houses are small, four room brick structures that have been built by the government to replace shanties, and the trend continues to where someday there will hopefully be no shantytowns left. There are park areas, a major hospital, local clinics and a new major shopping mall. No longer are residents restricted to having to live in such districts, and there are no longer any curfew laws, so Soweto residents can shop or dine in any part of the city they choose depending upon their income level. There are many thousands of residents who could afford to live in what were once white only communities, but prefer living in Soweto now by choice. It is still not totally safe for white people to tour around most parts of Soweto unaccompanied. But many tour companies do promote a group or private visit as a way to better understand the long history of oppression, especially during the Apartheid Era.

The central core of Johannesburg has the most concentrated number of high-rise office blocks and apartments of any city in the country. Although less favored as a venue within the white community, it is still patronized for various cultural or sporting events. The government has invested millions of Rand on having street surveillance cameras and added police presence in the downtown area. And as a result of these measures plus a stronger economy, crime rates are falling each year, but are still higher than in Cape Town or Durban. But downtown is no longer the core for the white population. Rosebank and Sandton are the two upmarket nodes located north of the city center, patronized by all cultural groups depending upon their income level. Sandton is the second largest commercial core in the entire metropolitan area, home to the largest shopping mall and some of the most expensive hotels and restaurants. The 2010 World Cup of soccer brought a lot of attention to Johannesburg, and a lot of money was spent in the improvement of the city's image.

North of Hillbrow are many formerly white only districts that developed at the turn of the 20th century. Victorian architecture for commercial and residential buildings, mostly utilizing brick with balustrades of wood or metal and ornate cornices is very reminiscent of the neighborhood architecture of Australian cities. The most fashionable residential district, one with large gated estates and streets where bowers meet overhead is Houghton. Here a mix of architectural styles can be seen. It is located to the east of Rosebank and north of the city center.

One characteristic of Johannesburg is the millions of trees that line city streets and are that are planted in parks and around private homes. This is an exceptionally green city, especially surprising on the High Veld where the natural cover is primarily grass. The city is also expanding and improving its parklands, adding to the overall beautification.

Because rural migrants and those from neighboring countries still hold the belief that their economic future awaits them in Johannesburg, there are squatter towns that have taken root on vacant land around the city. Unlike the former townships, these camps often have no running water, electricity or sanitary services. The municipal government is attempting to deal with this problem, but the influx of new migrants makes meaningful improvement almost impossible.

DEMOGRAPHICS: Over 70 percent of all residents in greater Johannesburg are Black Africans. The percentage, however, living today at middle or upper-middle income levels is the highest in history, and also the highest in the nation. This is the city of opportunity, and for some it has proven to be very meaningful.

The white population is only 16 percent of the urban total with Coloured standing at 6 percent and Asian at 4 percent.

English is the basic language of commerce and business in the city, Afrikaans being spoken by only around 7 percent of the population. The majority of Blacks speak tribal languages such as Zulu and Sotho both at home and on the streets, yet English still persists as the language of commerce whenever people of mixed races interact.

ECONOMY: Johannesburg is the financial and commercial heart of South Africa, and has the most diverse and viable economic base of any city on the continent. It is also the most modern and progressive large city in Africa.

Despite having been founded on gold, mining today is no longer king economically. The mines are among the deepest in the world because of the closer gold bearing strata having been worked out. Both gold and heavy metals processing and lighter manufacturing activities are found in Johannesburg. Mine headquarters are still a major factor in the city's financial life. Manufacturing has replaced gold mining as the most important economic activity. Trading in gold and diamonds still figures into the commercial and financial sectors of the Johannesburg. The city is the major center of banking and finance, and home to the largest stock exchange on the continent.

Johannesburg is the largest retail center in all of Africa. There are elegant shopping malls in Sandton, Melrose Arch and Rosebank. And there are other large middle-income shopping centers in every quadrant of the city.

The city is also the transport hub of the nation. It is the focus of the country's long distance expressways, the major railroad hub and the center of international aviation. A network of commuter rails and expressways serve the entire urban region. The newest project is the Gautrain, a new high-speed rail link between central Johannesburg, the international airport and Pretoria. It is only surpassed by the new Casablanca to Tangier high-speed train service in Morocco, which began in 2018.

WHERE TO STAY: For the benefit of readers who are planning to spend one or more nights in Johannesburg, this section will offer my evaluation of the best upmarket hotels in the city. The majority of hotels are located in the northern part of the city, as the downtown center is not recommended for foreign visitors based upon overall safety issues. The hotels I list below (alphabetically) are considered to be the finest in the city as well as the most secure. My choices are:

* AtholPlace Hotel & Villa – Located in Sandton at 90 Pretoria Avenue, this is a very elegant boutique property with elegantly furnished public and guest rooms. The hotel services include a restaurant, inclusive breakfast, room service, pool, spa, fitness center, concierge services and airport transportation. I GIVE IT *****

* Clico Boutique Hotel – Located in Rosebank at 27 Sturdee Avenue, this very fine boutique hotel offers a beautiful setting with a Cape Town Dutch designed building and lush landscaping. The hotel offers a well-known restaurant (see dining listing), room service, inclusive breakfast, pool, concierge service and airport transport. I GIVE IT *****

* Four Seasons Hotel – The Westcliff Johannesburg – Located in suburban Westcliff, this elegant hotel sits on magnificent landscaped grounds along the side of a hill with a sweeping view over the valley below. The hotel offers a fine restaurant, room service, banquet room, pool, spa and fitness center, business center, conference facilities, concierge, shuttle bus and airport transportation. I GIVE IT *****

* Hyatt Regency Johannesburg – At 191 Oxford Road in Rosebank, this is one of the best Hyatt Regency hotels you will find. The service and comfort ranks it higher among Hyatt properties to where it should be classed as a Grand Hyatt. The hotel offers dining facilities, room service, concierge, pool, fitness center, spa, meeting rooms and it also has a Club Level where breakfast and evening refreshments are included. Airport transport and guided tour services are available. I personally must note that it is my favorite Johannesburg property. I GIVE IT *****

* InterContinental Johannesburg – At the O. R. Tambo International Airport, this modern, high-rise hotel is convenient if you are just staying one night while en route to Kruger National Park or Cape Town. From the airport, you do have the Gautrain access to Sandton,

Rosebank and the city center. As a major hotel it offers dining facilities, room service, pool, fitness center, business center, meeting rooms and conference facilities. I GIVE IT ****

* Monarch Hotel – Conveniently located in Rosebank at 167 Oxford Road, this small but elegant hotel offers a restaurant, room service, inclusive breakfast, concierge, business center, conference facilities, but lacks a pool or fitness center. Airport transport is available. I GIVE IT ****

* Oasis Boutique Hotel – Located in beautiful Rivonia on the far northern edge of the city at 29 Homestead Road, this is a very beautiful and elegant small hotel. The property includes a pool, golf course access, restaurant, room service, inclusive breakfast, airport transportation but does not offer concierge or business services. And there is no fitness center. I GIVE IT ****

* Residence Boutique Hotel – Located in the elegant suburban district of Houghton, this small hotel offers the height of elegance and comfort. It is located at 17 Fourth Avenue, set amid beautiful grounds in a part of the city known for its magnificent large homes. All tariffs include a full breakfast. The hotel offers a dining room, room service, a pool, spa, fitness center, tennis courts, concierge service, meeting rooms, airport transportation and shuttle bus service. I GIVE IT *****

* Saxon Hotel Villas and Spa – In northern Sandhurst at 36 Saxon Road, this luxury hotel has a restaurant, room service, inclusive breakfast, banquet facilities, pool, spa, fitness center, concierge service and business center. Airport transportation is available. I GIVE IT *****

SIGHTSEEING FOR VISITORS: There are many sights in Johannesburg to keep a visitor busy for several days. Some cruise lines offer a pre or post cruise package whereby guests travel through Johannesburg to visit Kruger National Park, which is South Africa's premier game park. And on some of these itineraries a brief sightseeing excursion through Johannesburg is included.

Many cruise passengers will arrive from overseas by air through Johannesburg. As noted before, the vast majority will simply disembark and change planes to continue on to Cape Town. But those passengers who have done their homework and have read up on the city of Johannesburg will plan to stay for one or more days. I highly recommend that if your plans are to fly via Johannesburg that you should plan on at least two days, preferably more, to explore this complex and fascinating city.

* The most logical way to get around and also learn about the city and its people is to hire a car and driver/guide. Unlike many other large cities, the rates in Johannesburg are quite nominal. On average a full day will cost around 2,500.00 Rand, which is about $250.00 U.S. Dollars. Your hotel will be able to make arrangements, and when done by the concierge staff you can be assured of a competent professional. Driving on your own would not be recommended, as the city is too large and it is difficult to navigate because of the lack of a grid pattern once leaving the city center region. And remember that in South Africa, traffic

moves on the left, which for most Europeans and North Americans takes some getting accustomed to. And you would not want to accidentally wind up in some undesirable part of the city and not know how to extricate yourself.

* One private tour company that I do recommend is Tours by Locals. You can check their web page at www.toursbylocals.com for details about Johannesburg. But also compare what they offer with what your hotel concierge can provide.

* For group motor coach full day or half day tours that you can join to sightsee in and around Johannesburg and Pretoria, I recommend African Eagle. Check out their web page at www.daytours.co.za/tours/category/johannesburg-day-tours to see what they offer.

* Hop on hop off sightseeing busses are available in Johannesburg. There are two routes that the busses follow, and all of the stops are carefully chosen for maximum safety. There is also an additional route that visits the major venues in Soweto. For detailed information and a downloadable map, check on line at www.citysightseeing.co.za/johannesburg.

* I do not recommend taxis in Johannesburg except when ordered through your hotel concierge. If you use a taxi to sightsee or to dine out, be certain that return transportation is arranged in advance through the hotel. You do not want to become a victim of a crime by simply stepping into an unknown taxi.

WHAT TO SEE IN JOHANNESUBRG: I have divided the major sightseeing venues first into those that are in the city, followed by one-day outings into the High Veld where there are numerous fascinating game reserves and natural features. A discussion of Pretoria will follow in the next chapter, as being the national administrative capital; it is a city that needs to be treated separately.

The main venues in greater Johannesburg that I consider a must are (in alphabetical order) :
* Apartheid Museum - This is the most important museum in the city because it tells the story of Apartheid in all of its facets. Photographs, videos and artifacts describe in detail the racial policies that kept the people of South Africa segregated from one another from 1948 until 1991. And it tells the story of the struggle for independence. This museum is as much about the role of Nelson Mandela as it is about the Apartheid story. It is an absolute must. The museum is open daily from 9 AM to 5 PM. You should plan a minimum of two hours for your visit.

* Constitution Hill Human Rights Precinct - The Apartheid Era prisons and courts combined with an historical museum make this second in importance after the Apartheid Museum. This venue will bring home in full detail the indignities imposed by Apartheid. It is located above the city center and just west of Hillbrow at 11 Kotze Street. It is open daily from 9 AM to 5 PM and should be a must on your list of sights to see.

* FNB Stadium - Built for the 2010 World Cup, it was here that the public funeral service for Nelson Mandela was also held. It is the largest sports venue in South Africa with seating

for over 88,000 spectators. Tours of the stadium are given for groups and private individuals by advanced bookings at *functions@stadiummanagement.co.za* .

* Hillbrow – This is the most crime ridden part of Johannesburg that visitors should only take a walk through with their licensed guide. But a walk through Hillbrow shows you a side of urban life that is somewhat depressing, yet somewhat uplifting because of the attitude of its residents. Although poor, crime ridden and dangerous for outsiders, people who live in Hillbrow exhibit a pleasant disposition. If you visit with a guide, you will be welcomed.

* Johannesburg Botanical Gardens - For a chance to savor the cool and refreshing atmosphere of a beautiful park and garden, a visit here revitalizes, especially enjoyable on a warm day. The garden is located in suburban Randburg. It is open daily from 6 AM to 6 PM.

* Melrose Arch - This is the Johannesburg equivalent of what in the United States is known as Rodeo Drive in Beverly Hills, California. There is also excellent dining with live African entertainment available here. This center is north of the city center in suburban Melrose North and is a good place for high end shopping and elegant dining.

* Museum Africa - This museum tells the geographic and historic background of South Africa and once again places emphasis upon Apartheid. It is located in Newtown at 121 Lilian Ngoyi Avenue. The museum is open from 9 AM to 5 PM Tuesday thru Saturday.

* Sandton – Sandton is one of the most elegant neighborhoods in Johannesburg. It also contains a massive shopping, entertainment and hotel complexes where upmarket shopping, dining and conference facilities combine into a dazzling display of opulence. This is a good venue for extensive shopping, much of it high end. The mall also has many fine restaurants and is linked by high-speed train service to the International Airport and to Pretoria. The center is open Monday thru Saturday from 9 AM to 8 PM and on Sunday from 9 AM to 6 PM.

* South African National Museum of Military History - For those who love to see artillery, old airplanes and other items of war, this is an important venue. It is totally related to the military forces of South Africa. And again the role of the military during the anti-Apartheid uprisings is also told. The museum ios at 22 Eriswold Way and is open daily from 9 AM to 4:30 PM.

* Soweto - This largest of the former townships was home to Nelson Mandela and Bishop Desmond Tutu. There are important monuments to those martyrs in the struggle to end Apartheid plus the Mandela house that help further your insight into the country's past. And driving around in Soweto, you will see the vast improvements in the overall quality of life that are taking place today. Every visitor to Johannesburg should take a guided tour or come with a private car and driver/guide to this most famous of all the former Black African townships in the country.

* Top of Africa - Visit the rooftop observation deck some 50 stories above the city center at the Carlton Center. On a clear day you can see all of greater Johannesburg and the spine of the Witwatersrand. The view helps you to better visualize the size and scope of this massive urban community. The observation deck is open weekdays from 9 AM to 6 PM, Saturday from 9 AM to 5 PM and Sunday from 9 AM to 2 PM.

TOURS OUTSIDE OF THE CITY: If you have sufficient time and wish to explore the surrounding countryside, I recommend two long one-day outings that will be packed with sights to see and give you the feel for the High Veld. These include:

* Magaliesberg Mountains - With a driver/guide plan on spending the better part of a day driving out in the beautiful High Veld west of the city. First visit the Cradle of Humankind, which is today a UNESCO World Heritage site. It is located about 50 kilometers or 30 miles northwest of the city and open daily from 9 AM to 5 PM. Here you will see some of the archaeological diggings that have unearthed the oldest skeletons and artifacts of the first Homo sapiens. There is also the small Rhino and Lion Nature Reserve, which is part of the park complex. Then continue on to the Magaliesberg Protected Natural Area where you can enjoy the beautiful scenery of this small uplifted range. There are also beautiful villages and country towns such as Brits and Rustenberg where can have a chance to explore life in a rural community. You should plan upon this as a full day trip.

* Pilanesberg Game Reserve - This is a large provincial park and game reserve about two hours northwest of the city. If you are not staying long enough to visit Kruger National Park, here is an opportunity to visit an inland High Veld reserve where you have a chance to see the big 5 that many tourists believe is a must when coming to South Africa. You can book a trip to the Pilanesberg Game Reserve either through African Eagle, as noted earlier, at *www.daytours.co.za/tours/category/johannesburg-day-tours* or you can go on your own with a private car and driver/guide.

On the return you must stop for a couple of hours in Sun City. This is South Africa's prime resort in which gambling plays a major role. It is an all-purpose resort with a massive casino and architecture that will dazzle your senses. Sun City is bizarre and so out of character for the rest of the country. You should plan to spend the late afternoon and possibly stay for dinner at what is sometimes called the Las Vegas of Africa. Even if gaming is not of interest to you, just seeing this incredible resort is worth the stop. And their dining venues are excellent.

DINING OUT: The city of Johannesburg offers an incredible variety of dining establishments. They vary from what can be called fast food restaurants to very high end elegant dining rooms. I have chosen an assortment of medium to high end restaurants that are my favorites. It is impossible to capture every aspect of dining in the city. I have placed special emphasis upon restaurants in the more up market parts of the city that also specialize in South African cuisine along with Continental. All of my listings are shown alphabetically and I have weeded out those where at least ten percent of those who have written reviews gave the restaurant less than average marks unless my own personal experience said otherwise. One problem in Johannesburg is that so many restaurants appear to be great, but they are not consistent and end up with mixed reviews. I have avoided those in all cases. My listings include:

* Bellgables Country Restaurant – For a chance to dine on the High Veld just outside of the city, this is a delightful and popular restaurant. It is northwest of the city in Muldersdrift and a visit could be combined with a trip out to the Magaliesberg Mountains. The menu is quite broad and is essentially Continental but does feature Vegetarian dishes as well as a range of meats, poultry and seafood. The menu can best be described as very elegant and the cuisine is beautifully presented. A visit on the way back from the mountains is a nice way to end the day. Hours of service are Thursday thru Sunday lunch from Noon on and dinner Wednesday thru Saturday from 7 PM. No set closing hours are stated. Reservations are essential.

* Bread and Roses Café and Bistro – In Melville at 80 Fourth Avenue, this is a very popular local café that has a great international menu and also offers vegetarian friendly fare. Their sandwiches and cheese plates are very popular, as are their breakfast offerings. Sunday brunch is also well attended by local diners. Hours of service are from 7:30 AM to 6 PM weekdays and from 8 AM to 6 PM on weekends.

* Chaplin's Grill – Located in Hurlingham Manor at 61 Woodlands Avenue, this restaurant is just a short distance northwest of Sandton Centre. It has a fine reputation for its grilled beef, chicken ostrich, venison, lamb, pork, duck and seafood. With starters, salads and sides, there is something to satisfy every taste. They are open weekdays from Noon to 2:30 PM for lunch and 6 to 10 PM for dinner. Saturday dinner is served from 6 to 10 PM. Reservations are recommended for dinner.

* Clico Restaurant – In Rosebank at 27 Sturdee Avenue, this is a very elegant dining room that is part of a boutique hotel of equal elegance. The restaurant serves Continental, Vegetarian and Vegan dishes all expertly prepared and beautifully served. The atmosphere is very conducive to a relaxing meal. Dishes are seasonal and only the freshest ingredients are used. All three meals are served, and this is a nice change of pace for breakfast if you are in Rosebank. Hours of service are from 7 AM to 10 PM daily. Reservations are advised for lunch or dinner.

* Cuisine Afrique – Located in the Afrique Boutique Hotel in Boksburg, which is west of the city center of Johannesburg. This is a gem of a restaurant where the menu includes a wide array of tempting starters, salads, mains that range from meat to poultry and seafood and there are elegant desserts at the end of the meal. There are also vegetarian dishes on the menu as well. Hours of service are Monday thru Saturday from 6:30 AM to 10 PM and Sunday from 7 AM to 4 PM. Reservations are recommended.

* Fishmonger (Illovo) – Located in Thrupps Centre in suburban Illovo, this is a well-recognized seafood restaurant. Fresh catch prepared in a Mediterranean style is the rule, and the dishes are beautifully presented. Illovo is just north of Rosebank and close to most major hotels. The restaurant is open from Noon to 10:30 PM daily. Reservations are advised for dinner.

* Grillhouse Sandton – Located at 11 Alice Lane Precinct in Sandton, this is a restaurant where the fired grill sizzles as steaks, chops and fish are prepared to order. Meat is the specialty so vegetarians be warned. The quality of the meals combined with a casual indoor-outdoor atmosphere make this a favorite with locals. They are open daily from Noon to 10 PM and reservations are advised for evenings.

* House of Baobab – Located in Mabobeng Precinct, Kruger Street in the city center of Johannesburg, this is real African experience with cuisine that will wow the most skeptical of diners. It receives rave reviews from tourists and locals alike for its innovative way of introducing a cuisine that is so representative of South Africa's heritage. There are vegetarian dishes on the menu. The restaurant is open Tuesday thru Sunday from Noon to 10 PM and a reservation is advised.

* Les Delices de France – This is an elegant restaurant with gracious service and Continental cuisine in the French manner. It is located at the corner of Gordon Road and Keith Avenue in suburban Rooodepoort, which is in the southwestern part of the city some distance from Rosebank or Sandton. The overall ambiance is that of Europe and it is a welcome change of pace when on the go and doing a lot of sightseeing during the day. Lunch is served Tuesday thru Friday from Noon to 3 PM and it is conveniently located if you are visiting Soweto in the morning. Dinner is served Tuesday thru Saturday from 6:30 to 10 PM. Lunch is only served on Sunday from Noon to 3 PM. Reservations should be made.

* Licorish Bistro – Located in suburban Bryanston at 432 Nicolway, this restaurant features European and Continental cuisine served in a casual atmosphere. The dishes are expertly prepared and served by friendly waiters. The restaurant receives strong reviews from both locals and visitors. It is open Monday, Tuesday, Thursday and Friday from 8 AM to 10:30 PM. Wednesday and Saturday it opens at 9 PM and stays open until 10:30 PM. Sunday hours are from 9 AM to 4 PM.

* Lucky Bean – Located at 16 Seventh Street in Melville, this is a restaurant that specializes in traditional African and Continental cuisine, served in a subtle and beautiful setting. The menu is diverse, the service excellent and the atmosphere conducive to a delightful experience. The restaurant is open Tuesday thru Sunday from 11 AM to Midnight and reservations are advised.

* Moyo Melrose Arch – This is one of my favorite restaurants for a combination of traditional African cuisine along with strolling musicians that add to the overall African ambiance. The menu includes dishes from all parts of sub Saharan Africa, including meats, poultry and seafood. I have never been anything less than pleased by the friendly atmosphere and good food. If the strolling musicians stop at your table, a small gratuity is expected. Moyo is open daily from 11 AM to 11 PM. Reservations should be made for the dinner hour.

* Ocean Basket Sunninghill – On Rivona Road, Shop 16-17, this is the best loved of the various Ocean Basket restaurant chain locations in Johannesburg. This nationwide chair varies in the quality of each local venue. But this one does shine. It is a moderately priced

family oriented restaurant serving excellent seafood dishes. I have eaten at Ocean Basket restaurants in several South African cities, and this one is very good. They are open daily from 10:30 AM, closing at 9:30 PM Sunday thru Thursday and at 10 PM Friday and Saturday.

* Robby's Place – Here is a chance to dine in Soweto and experience South African cuisine served in the most infamous of the former Apartheid Era townships. Robby's Place is located at 5634 Mokoka Street in Pimville, Soweto. This is a dining experience like no other. You will sample the traditional flavors of Black Africa in a very warm and friendly atmosphere. The restaurant is open weekdays from 10 AM to 10 PM and on weekends from 10 AM to 2 AM. It is especially lively on weekends.

* Salvation Café – This very casual bistro is located just north of the city center in Millpark at 44 Stanley Avenue. It is a popular local eatery that has a great vibe according to locals. The menu is Continental and International. The meals are well prepared and served with guests wanting to come back for more. They have both a café menu and a deli menu to give diners the widest array possible. They are open daily from 8 AM to 5 PM.

* Yeoville Dinner Club – 24 Rockey Street in Yeoville, which is just northeast of the Johannesburg city center, this is a grand pan African experience. The menu is a tour d'force of the African continent. The best way to describe the menu is to say that it is exotic. You will be introduced to dishes of amazing flavor and I doubt if you will leave without a feeling of great satisfaction. It is actually hard to describe the variety of dishes presented. There are pickles, melons, grains, beans, fish, roasted meats and more served at communal tables. This is a restaurant to be experienced. They are open Tuesday thru Saturday from 6 to 11 PM and on Sunday from 2 to 6 PM for lunch. Reservations are advised.

FINAL WORDS: I have prepared a separate chapter on Pretoria even though the two cities have almost merged into one gigantic metropolis. Pretoria is distinctly different and deserving of a separate listing.

Johannesburg is slowly overcoming the negative publicity it has received in the past two decades for its crime and violence. Yes it is a city in which you need to be careful, and it is preferable to always have a guide when going around to explore. But with a guide, most often who is Black African, you will be able to see the city in a totally different light. You will see both the good and the not so good, or frankly bad areas, but you will be safe in doing so. It is quite an eye opener to visit this massive city with its many layers of ethnic diversity that was once reserved exclusively for the white elite during the Apartheid Era. Today Johannesburg is coming of age and it is a fascinating city to explore.

JOHANNESBURG MAPS

THE CENTRAL CITY OF JOHANNESBURG

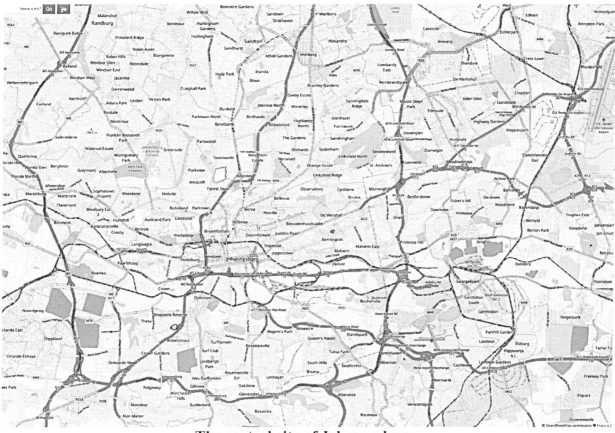

The central city of Johannesburg

This map is best viewed directly from OpenStreetMap.com on your personal device where it can be expanded or one specific area can be enlarged. Given the format of this book, it is impossible to display maps with the level of detail you might wish to have while actually out exploring the city. But the OpenStreetMap maps used directly are the tool I always rely upon.

THE VAST SUBURB OF SOWETO

The former township and now vast suburb of Soweto

This map is best viewed directly from OpenStreetMap.com on your personal device where it can be expanded or one specific area can be enlarged. Given the format of this book, it is impossible to display maps with the level of detail you might wish to have while actually out exploring the city. But the OpenStreetMap maps used directly are the tool I always rely upon.

THE COMMERCIAL HEART OF JOHANNESBURG

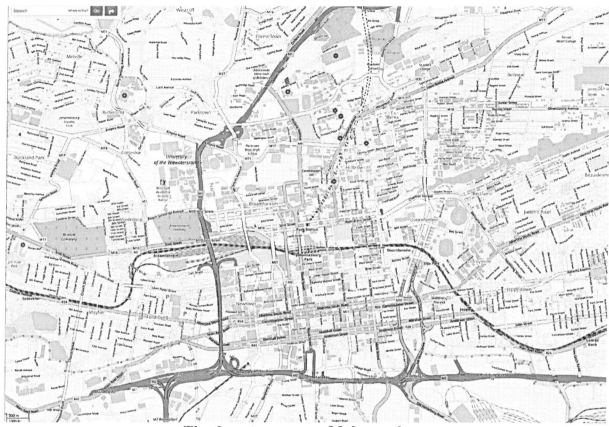

The downtown core of Johannesburg

This map is best viewed directly from OpenStreetMap.com on your personal device where it can be expanded or one specific area can be enlarged. Given the format of this book, it is impossible to display maps with the level of detail you might wish to have while actually out exploring the city. But the OpenStreetMap maps used directly are the tool I always rely upon.

THE NORTHERN SUBURBS OF ROSEBANK AND MELROSE

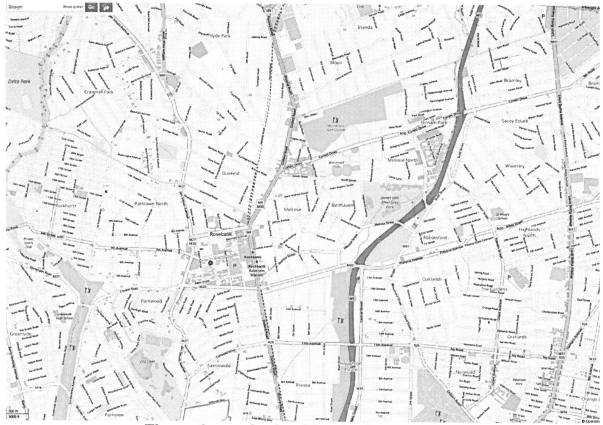

The northern suburbs of Rosebank and Melrose

This map is best viewed directly from OpenStreetMap.com on your personal device where it can be expanded or one specific area can be enlarged. Given the format of this book, it is impossible to display maps with the level of detail you might wish to have while actually out exploring the city. But the OpenStreetMap maps used directly are the tool I always rely upon.

THE NORTHERN SUBURB OF SANDTON

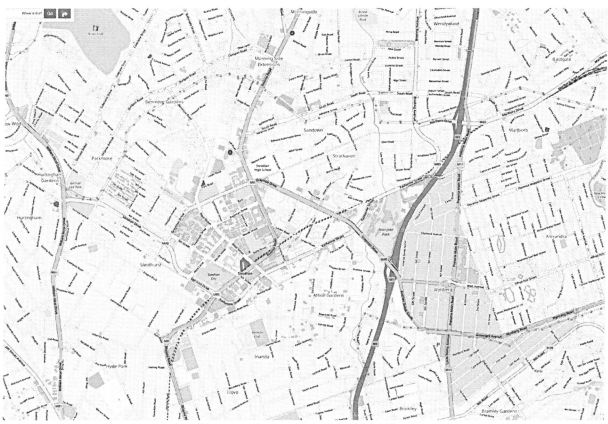

The northern suburb of Sandton

This map is best viewed directly from OpenStreetMap.com on your personal device where it can be expanded or one specific area can be enlarged. Given the format of this book, it is impossible to display maps with the level of detail you might wish to have while actually out exploring the city. But the OpenStreetMap maps used directly are the tool I always rely upon.

Flying over Soweto on approach to Johannesburg from the west

Looking north into central Johannesburg from the plane

Low over an upscale suburb on approach to the airport

The heart of the city from the Carlton Centre 50th floor

Looking south from the Carlton Centre 50th floor to the Witwatersrand goldfields

Looking north toward Houghton from the Carlton Centre 50th floor

The heart of downtown Johannesburg in Cenotaph Square

Outside of Park Street Station in the heart of downtown

In the heart of Hillbrow adjacent to downtown Johannesburg

Hillbrow is very animated and colorful and friendly when you are with a guide

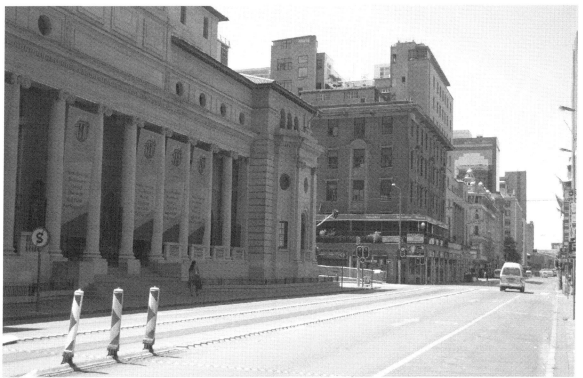
City Hall in downtown Johannesburg

Outside the Apartheid Museum, as no photos allowed inside

A tribute to Nelson Mandela at the Apartheid Museum

The house where Nelson Mandela lived in Soweto before his arrest

The monument to fallen children during the Soweto uprisings

Modern housing replacing shanties in Soweto

In the main commercial hub of Soweto

Kliptown is still a shantytown, (Work of Rachel, CC BY SA 2.0, Wikimedia.org)

In the beautiful and green Houghton District

On the green streets of Houghton

The Rosebank Mall courtyard

Upmarket Melrose Arch shopping district

In upmarket Sandton

Nelson Mandela Square in Sandton

In the Cradle of Humankind UNESCO World Heritage Site

The High Veld in the Cradle of Humankind

Crossing the border into the province of North West

Harsbeespoort Lake on the edge of the Magaliesberg Mountains

The Crocodile River in the Magaliesberg Mountains

An arts and crafts center in the Magaliesberg Mountains

In Pilanesberg National Park, (Work of NJR ZA, CC BY SA 3.0, Wikimedia.org)

The Palace at Sun City in North West province, (South African Tourism, CC BY SA 2.0, Wikimedia.org)

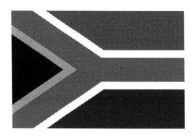

THE NATIONAL CAPITAL
PRETORIA

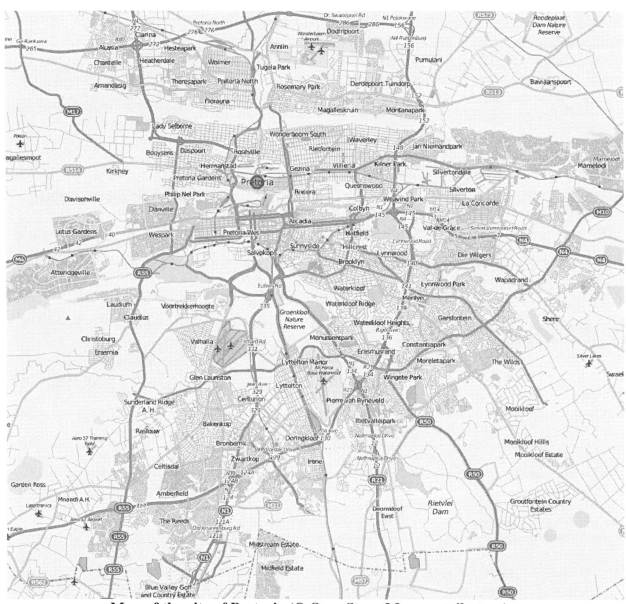

Map of the city of Pretoria (© OpenStreetMap contributors)

There are a few countries in the world that divide up their federal government and have two national capital cities, but South Africa is the only country in the world that officially has three national capital cities, each serving a specific function. Pretoria is the administrative capital of South Africa. This implies that the President and all high-ranking government officials have their offices here, as do all the various governmental departments and agencies. Likewise, foreign governments that have diplomatic relations with South Africa maintain their embassies in Pretoria. The South African Parliament holds its sessions in Cape Town and the Supreme Court of South Africa sits in Bloemfontein. But Pretoria is recognized as the primary capital.

Located just 56 kilometers or 35 miles north of the heart of Johannesburg, Pretoria is a totally separate city. The outer suburbs of both major cities have almost joined, but there is still a bit of open countryside between the two great urban centers. The metropolitan population of Pretoria is 1,736,000 and this excludes any outer suburbs that are claimed as part of metropolitan Johannesburg. The new and fast Gautrain along with a multi-lane express highway links the two cities. It is therefore possible to live in the suburbs of one city and work in the other. The Gautrain only takes 25 minutes from downtown Johannesburg to downtown Pretoria.

The population matrix of Pretoria is different from any other city in the country because 52 percent of the urban population is white European while only 42 percent is Black African. The Coloured and Asian populations are exceptionally small at 2.5 and 1.9 percent respectively. The Afrikaans language is still the primary language of 48 percent of the population, reflecting the Boer heritage of the city, as it was the capital of the Transvaal Republic before the second Boer War. And during the hated years of Apartheid, few jobs for Black Africans were available in government, the majority being reserved for white Afrikaners and that is why the high percentage of whites in the city. Also taken into account are the thousands of foreign nationals who work at the embassies of the nations represented to South Africa through their diplomatic missions.

PHYSICAL SETTING: When traveling from Johannesburg to Pretoria there is a decrease of 366 meters or 1,200 feet in elevation, as the city sits in a valley between moderately high east to west ridges that are an extension of the Magaliesberg Mountains. As you travel north of the city, the land continues to decrease in elevation from the High Veld into what is considered a more savanna-like environment called the Bushveld.

The climate is slightly warmer and more subtropical than that of Johannesburg partly because of its lower elevation, but also due to its sheltered location between the two mountain ridges. Summers and winters are both a few degrees warmer. Frost is less likely than in Johannesburg during winter, and there is no recorded event of snowfall while Johannesburg has a bit of snow every few years.

BRIEF HISTORY: Prior to the coming of the Dutch Voortrekkers, the history of the region is long. Recall my mentioning the Cradle of Mankind, the oldest known site for Homo sapiens. The national park is just due southwest of Pretoria. This area therefore has a long human history. Ultimately the Bantu tribes arrived in the 13th century and have struggled among one another for dominance over the region. When the Dutch began their expansion eastward into Zulu territory, the Zulu expanded northward, displacing the Swazi and other tribes.

The Dutch or Boer trek inland to the Transvaal occurred in the mid 19th century. It was Marthinus Pretorius, one of the Voortrekker leaders, who founded the city in 1855, naming it for his late father who was the victor in the Battle of Blood River with the Zulu. Pretoria became the capital of the Transvaal Republic, and a stronghold for Afrikaner independence. The British tried to coerce the Orange Free State and Transvaal into a union similar to the Anglo French union of Canada, but the Dutch were not amenable to such a relationship, especially with the newly found wealth of diamonds in Kimberley. What brought matters to a head was the British victory over the Zulu, with Voortrekker aid, leading to the British declaring that the Transvaal and Orange Free State territories were now annexed. The first Boer War broke out and the conflict lasted from December 1880 to March 1881, ending with British recognition of the South African Republic that included the Orange Free State and Transvaal.

After gold was discovered in the Witwatersrand and Johannesburg began to flourish, there were added tensions between the British and the South African Republic. Tensions led to the Second Boer War that lasted from 1899 to 1902 and ended with the South African Republic being united with the Cape Colony and Natal to form the Union of South Africa in 1910. The complexities of the war would take up a whole chapter, most of which would not relate to the city of Pretoria. During both Boer Wars, Pretoria was a major target because it was the stronghold of the Afrikaners who wanted a separate nation. After the war, the new union was given its multiple capital cities as a means of placating the Dutch, thus Pretoria became the administrative capital of the new unified nation. And Bloemfontein, also an Afrikaaner stronghold, became the judicial capital while Cape Town, which was heavily dominated by the British, became the legislative capital. And so it remains that way today.

During the Apartheid Era, Pretoria was the stronghold of the leadership that brought all the hated restrictions into force. There were few menial jobs open to Blacks in the capital, and the city remained exclusively white. Only a few townships existed on the outer fringes of the city. With the end of Apartheid and the first free election in 1994, Blacks now came to power in both the Parliament and Cabinet. Thus today there is a healthy mix of black and white residents in Pretoria to where there is nearly an equal balance.

In most recent years, the African National Congress has attempted to change many place names to reflect a more African heritage. But the Afrikaners have voiced strong objection to the proposed name Tshwane for Pretoria, saying it denies their right to the historical heritage of the city. As a compromise, the Metropolitan Municipality that includes Pretoria is now known as Tshwane, but the city remains as Pretoria.

SIGHTS TO SEE: The major historic and cultural sights of Pretoria can easily be seen in one day. Therefore it is not necessary to pack up and change hotels from Johannesburg to Pretoria. My recommendation is to have your Johannesburg hotel make arrangements for a driver/guide in Pretoria to meet you at the end of the Gautrain line. By taking the train from either Rosebank or Sandton, you will arrive in approximately 20 minutes, and this gives you an opportunity to ride this new high-speed rail system. Most of the major hotels are located very close to either station, or a short distance away. And hotels generally have a shuttle car that can both take you to the station and pick you up upon your return. The alternative is to simply use your driver/guide from Johannesburg and travel via the express highway.

If should be taking the Blue Train at the end of your cruise and coming north to Johannesburg, you will end your rail journey in Pretoria. But the best hotels, restaurants and majority of the sights are in Johannesburg and most hotels will arrange transport from the Blue Train into the city. You should still spend one day and come back to Pretoria because there are sights worthy of your time.

* I strongly urge you to use a private car and driver/guide for your visit to Pretoria. It may cost more but it gives you the convenience of pick up at your hotel and the flexibility of seeing the city at your leisure.

* There are a few tours from Johannesburg that spend the day in Pretoria, but you lose time in arranging to meet the motor coach before leaving Johannesburg and then again having to arrange a drop off back at your hotel. But if you insist on taking a group tour, check out the web page of Rhino Africa at www.rhinoafrica.com for information on their half day tour to Pretoria.

Here is my recommendation for the major sights to see in Pretoria during a one-day visit (shown in alphabetical order):

* Freedom Park – Located at Koch Street and Seventh Avenue in suburban Salvokop, this magnificent park is filled with monuments dedicated to the history of South Africa, especially the struggle for universal suffrage and the end to Apartheid. It is an absolute must when visiting Pretoria. The park is open from 9 AM to 4 PM daily.

* Church Square - The heart of the city of Pretoria, this square is surrounded by many historic buildings from the Dutch and later British 19th century, including many formerly important government buildings. Although the square is often crowded, it is worth parking and walking through the square and around its perimeter to get the flavor and vibe of downtown Pretoria.

* Fort KlapperKop Heritage Site - An interesting hilltop museum in a onetime military fort that was designed to defend Pretoria against riots or demonstrations. It also has great views over the city. The focus of the exhibits is the Boer War period. The museum is open Tuesday thru Sunday from 10 AM to 5 PM.

* National Cultural History Museum - This museum at 121 Visagi Street in central Pretoria is one of the hidden gems of the city. Its focus is on cultural history not only of South Africa, but has exhibits from many world regions. The museum is open daily from 8 AM to 4 PM.

* **National Union Buildings** - This is the national administrative capital building of the country. The distinctively designed buildings with an Italian renaissance style sits on a high hill overlooking the city and the terrace in front of the main entry has great views over the city. The landscaped grounds are also quite beautiful and the big attraction is the open arms statue of Nelson Mandela that now greets visitors coming up the sweeping staircase to the front of the buildings. Tours of the interior of the buildings are generally not offered.

* **Pretoria Art Museum** - This museum, located in suburban Arcadia, has a superb collection of South African artists, including those who are contemporary. The museum is open Tuesday thru Sunday from 10 AM to 5 PM.

* **Pretoria National Botanical Garden** - A beautiful garden with a collection of plants and flowers representative of South Africa. The garden is located in suburban Brummeria, and is one of the most beautiful of public gardens in the country. The garden is open daily from 8 AM to 6 PM.

* **South African Air Force Museum** - This museum is for those who have a great love of airplanes and are interested in the historic role of the South African Air Force, one of the strongest on the continent. The museum is on the Swartkop Air Force Base, which allows access to visitors just for the museum grounds and building. In 2018 the museum was closed because of reconstructive work on the base. It is expected to reopen sometime in 2019 thus it is recommended to check before attempting to visit. The web page is _www.saafmuseum.org.za._ Normal hours when open are Wednesday thru Saturday from 10 AM to 3 PM.

* **Voortrekker Monument and Heritage Site** - This is a monument dedicated to the original Dutch settlement of Pretoria. It is located atop a major hill south of the city and has excellent views of the city, looking back toward the Union Building. This is considered to be an almost sacred site by Afrikaners. The monument is open daily from 8 AM to 5 PM and is usually visited when coming from Johannesburg before entering the city.

If you are spending more than a day in Pretoria, or wish to return for more of an out of doors adventure, there are several recommended natural preserves around the city worthy of note. These include:

* **Ann van Dyk Cheetah Center** – The center is located off route R 519 outside of Pretoria. Here is an opportunity to learn about the cheetah and get up close to these elusive big cats. Morning is the best time, as the cats are quiet in the afternoon hours, The center is open daily from 9 AM to 5 PM.

* **Groenkloof Nature Reserve** - Close to the city, this rather hilly reserve just south of the city offers mountain biking and nature walks. Its animal life includes many giraffe, kudu, zebra, antelope and other herd animals. It is a safe venue for walking, as there are no big cats to worry about being attacked. The reserve opens at 5:30 AM and closes at 7 PM daily. It is only about a one hour drive or less from the northern suburbs of Johannesburg where most major hotels are located.

* Rietvlei Nature Reserve - Not well known to foreign visitors, this reserve is close to the city, located to the southeast and actually just as close to the northern suburbs of Johannesburg and can be reached in an hour or less driving time. It affords an opportunity to see lions, rhinos and other big game animals by self-driving or guided tours. They also offer evening guided tours when lions tend to be more active. The reserve is open from 5:30 AM to 7 PM daily.

DINING OUT: If you plan to spend a day in Pretoria and have come with your own private car and driver/guide, you will no doubt want to take time out for lunch. I list below three good restaurant choices that offer both the local flavor and color that will help to make your visit more meaningful. I have chosen these restaurants based both upon their cuisine and atmosphere as well as their overall quality. As in Johannesburg, so many of the restaurants are inconsistent in their quality and service. My choices are (shown alphabetically):

* La Terrasse Rooftop Café and Deli – Located at 435 Atterbury Road just east of the city center, this restaurant specializes in North African cuisine with a strong emphasis upon the delectable spices of Morocco. It also features dishes from elsewhere on the African continent and is a very popular local restaurant, which gives you a true sample of what is loved by people in Pretoria. They are open Monday thru Saturday from 9 AM to 5 PM.

* Mo Zam Bik Silver Lake k- Just east of the city center at the corner of N 4 Highway and Hans Strydom Drive in Silver Lake, this restaurant offers the tastes of neighboring Mozambique, the country to the northeast of South Africa. And the influencing factor is that of the country's former Portuguese colonial heritage. There is a strong emphasis upon fresh seafood prepared with both African and Portuguese traditions combined into a unique menu. Chicken and beef dishes are also a part of the rather extensive menu, which you will find quite tempting. Lunch is served Monday thru Saturday starting at Noon and on Sunday starting at 11 AM. The restaurant closes at 10 PM Monday thru Thursday and at 11 PM on Friday and Saturday but closes at 5 PM Sunday.

* Pachas Restaurant – Just east of the city center at 22 Dely Road in Hazelwood, this is a very popular restaurant with a rather broad menu that is quite international. And the restaurant is also known for its fine quality grilled meats. The menu features a variety of hot or cold starters, salads, grilled meats, poultry and seafood so that there is something for everyone. They are open Monday thru Saturday from Noon to 10 PM and Sunday for lunch only Noon to 3 PM.

FINAL WORDS: As the national capital and a city with a rich Afrikaans history, this is a city not to be missed when staying over at least two to three days in Johannesburg. Population wise it is the fourth largest city in South Africa, but it is slowly merging with Johannesburg, as the suburbs of both cities grow closer together.

Pretoria is also a beautiful city to spend a bit of time driving around, especially in the spring when the jacaranda trees are flowering. This is one of the most popular trees heavily planted throughout the city, although it is originally native to eastern Australia. In summer the city's leafy green canopy and stately homes makes visiting its residential districts quite worthwhile. For its overall population, Pretoria has fewer of the unsightly former townships since until the end of the Apartheid Era it was essentially off limits to the Black African population. But of course today it is the administrative capital of a multi-racial nation that no longer has the repressive laws of racial separation. But unfortunately the unequal economics of a multi-racial society still present problems in the development of full integration, similar in many ways to that of the United States, but more pronounced due to the recency of the emergency of the country from Apartheid.

PRETORIA MAPS

THE CITY OF PRETORIA

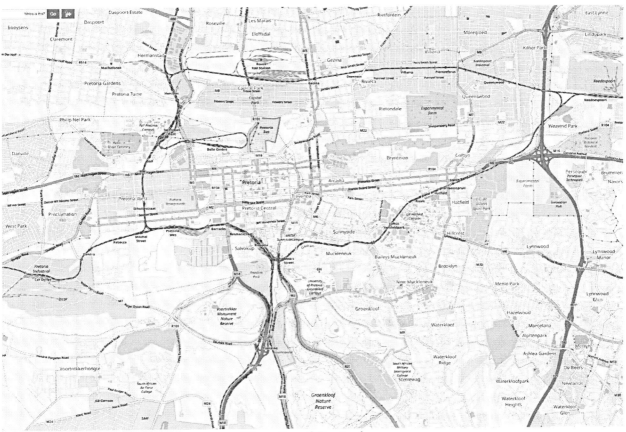

The city of Pretoria

This map is best viewed directly from OpenStreetMap.com on your personal device where it can be expanded or one specific area can be enlarged. Given the format of this book, it is impossible to display maps with the level of detail you might wish to have while actually out exploring the city. But the OpenStreetMap maps used directly are the tool I always rely upon.

THE COMMERCIAL HEART OF PRETORIA

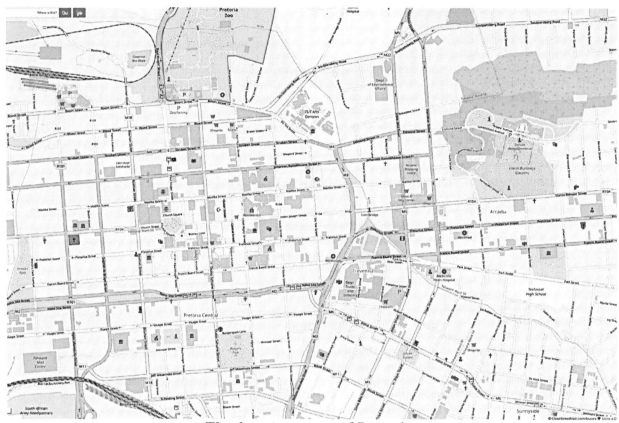

The downtown core of Pretoria

This map is best viewed directly from OpenStreetMap.com on your personal device where it can be expanded or one specific area can be enlarged. Given the format of this book, it is impossible to display maps with the level of detail you might wish to have while actually out exploring the city. But the OpenStreetMap maps used directly are the tool I always rely upon.

The Gautrain at one of the intermediate suburban stations north of Johannesburg

Passing a former township near Midrand

The Gautrain arrival in Pretoria

Looking over the heart of Pretoria from the National Union Buildings

A second view of the heart of Pretoria to the left of the view above

The statue of Nelson Mandela looks over the grounds of the National Union Building

The statue of Nelson Mandela welcomes all to the National Union Buildings

Preamble to the Constitution of South Africa at the Union Building

Church Square in downtown Pretoria

Paul Kruger Street in downtown Pretoria

The South Africa National Museum

The South Africa Museum

A typical leafy green Pretoria street

With a large civil service population Pretoria has numerous apartment blocks

NAMIBIA AS A NATION

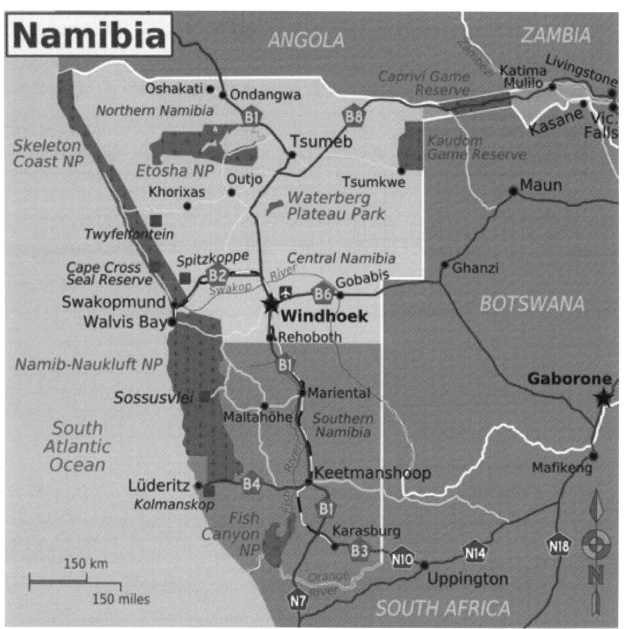

Map of the regions of Namibia (Work of NJR ZA & Shaundd, CC BY SA 3.0, Wikimedia.org)

Most cruise itineraries around South Africa include a detour north along the Atlantic coast to the Republic of Namibia, formerly known as South West Africa. Namibia is a large country with a very small population. The land area encompasses 825,428 square kilometers or 318.696 square miles, making it the size of the Canadian province of British Columbia. The population of Namibia is only 2,587,00 at the last estimate in 2018. Based upon its land area, only Mongolia has a lower population density than Namibia.

Half of the population is Bantu speaking, but comprised of several tribes with the Ovambo being the largest group, accounting for half of the Bantu people in the country. In addition, there is the Khoisan, including the Nama and San people. We know them better as the Bushmen and Hottentot. The white European population of Namibia is around 14 percent of the total. They are a mix of descendants of the original German settlers, Dutch Afrikaners and Portuguese.

NATURAL LANDSCAPE: Namibia is the most arid nation in southern Africa. It contains two distinct desert regions that merge together to occupy the bulk of the country. It is the latitude range and being situated on the west coast of southern Africa that account for the country's aridity.

The Namib Desert is a flat, very sandy coastal desert that results from the Benguela Current in the South Atlantic Ocean. This very cold current flowing north out of Antarctic waters inhibits the evaporation as warm air moves from sea toward land. The warm air is chilled by the ocean, its limited moisture condensing out at coastal fog. It is from this fog and accompanying dew that the limited plant life derives its water. The northern portion of the Namib Desert is often called the Skeleton Coast because of past shipwrecks leading to the crews dying from thirst in a desert that is the driest on earth.

Inland from the Namib Desert and separated physically by the Great Escarpment of the Central Plateau, the land first rises abruptly and then descends slightly to a highland plateau that averages 1,200 to 1,500 meters or 4,000 to 5,000 feet in elevation. It highest point is along the escarpment at Königstein, which is 2,606 meters or 8,550 feet high. The plateau is cooler because of its elevation, but it is still essentially a desert in the south and grades into a savanna in the north where it receives a slight amount of summer rainfall that spreads inland across the narrower lower part of the continent from the Indian Ocean. The escarpment in the south also receives limited summer rainfall, as the high wall squeezes out what moisture reaches inland coming off the colder waters of the Atlantic Ocean.

The only part of Namibia that is classed as humid is the Bushveld in the far northeast. This area receives almost 419 millimeters or 16 inches of rain, mainly in the summer. To the south and east, the Bushveld gives way to the Kalahari Desert. But unlike the Namib, the Kalahari does receive on average 250 to 380 millimeters or 10 to 15 inches of rain per year, mainly during the summer monsoons that penetrate across from the Indian Ocean. The desert is rich in plant life, containing a wide variety of succulent vegetation. To be succulent, a plant must be capable of storing water in its flesh. All cacti are succulents, but all succulents are not cacti. The various plants of the Kalahari are unique to this area, but they are not cacti. There are over 5,000 species in the wettest part of the Kalahari, making this a rich and distinctive desert. For clarification, cacti are only found in the Western Hemisphere as native species. Ranchers have introduced cacti to the desert fringes of North Africa and in a few isolated parts of the Kalahari Desert.

The landscapes of Namibia are quite beautiful. There are many areas of red to rust colored rock that outcrops in the form of massive crags, cliffs or mesas. The vegetation cover is scant, but still adds touches of green. Along the coast you will see the world's largest sand dunes, the result of onshore winds piling up the eroded debris of tens of thousands of years. Small canyons have been gouged into the escarpment and in these you find a variety of trees that grow along streams that only carry water during the brief wet season. Yet the roots can be moistened by capillary action from deep underground.

Namibia has a surprising amount of wildlife, even in the apparently desolate Namib Desert. There is an elephant species that has adapted to the desert conditions in the north. And there are lions and other predators out on the Kalahari Desert. Grazing animals, which form the prey, also survive on the meager food sources. Parts of northern Namibia and neighboring Botswana support large numbers of animals, especially where inland waterways travel from the more humid east and loose themselves in the deserts and savannas. The most famous is the Etosha Plain and the great Okavango Delta in neighboring Botswana. The Etosha is a massive salty plain of interior drainage. During the wet season, small rivers drain into it, creating a shallow saline lake that attracts many herd animals and predators who migrate into the region following the summer moisture.

Namibia is a hot country. The Sub Tropical High Pressure system that spins counterclockwise descends over Namibia and keeps the country very warm and cloudless. But during the high sun or summer, the high moves south and enables tropical rain showers to penetrate into the country, primarily benefitting the north. But along the coast, fog is the main source of moisture with the on shore flow of steady breezes. But during the dry lower sun season there are occasions when the descending and warming air off the escarpment is so strong as to create sandstorms over the Namib Desert.

Fortunately the low population and limited agriculture of Namibia enable the population to survive. Groundwater is the main source for domestic uses, as the sub surface aquifers are able to recharge from the limited precipitation and deep underground movements down from the wetter north.

A BRIEF HISTORY: The key to understanding Namibia's history can be seen in its place names. It was the German colonial era that led to exploration and the naming of rivers, mountains and other natural features. Germans founded most Namibian towns. Thus German nomenclature gives an outward clue as to the country's European historic connection.

The earliest known European to visit was the Portuguese explorer Diego Cão in 1485, followed by Bartolomeu Dias a year later. But like in South Africa, the Portuguese never laid claim to any of southern Africa. The land was left alone for centuries, as its hostile coastline was not conducive to explorations farther inland.

In 1874 the first group of German and Swedish trekkers came from the Trnsvaal en route to Angola seeking new settlement opportunities, crossing Namibia in its northeast corner. Eventually a few settled in the highlands after finding life under Portuguese rule unacceptable. But it was not until 1884 that Imperial Germany laid claim to South West Africa, fearing the British may annex this last unclaimed piece of real estate. But the British did manage to seize Walvis Bay, since it was the only significant anchorage along the entire coast.

Resistance from local Herero and Namaqua tribes against German troops resulted in near genocide for both groups. Those who survived were forced into servitude, barred from returning to their lands or made to flee. In essence the Germans were brutal in their occupation, far worse than the indignities forced upon Blacks by the Dutch or British in South Africa. Some historians have gone as far as to say that Hitler may have used the extermination and repression in Namibia as a model for Nazi treatment of Jews in Germany starting in the 1930's.

After their defeat in World War I, Germany was forced to surrender its overseas colonial holdings in the South Pacific and Africa to the League of Nations. In 1919, South Africa was given a mandate by the League to administer South West Africa, as their troops had been instrumental in forcing German troops to surrender during the war. South Africa did not officially absorb South West Africa, keeping the facade of mandated caretaker, but for all practical purposes, they did incorporate it into the Union with white representation in their Parliament.

When the United Nations replaced the League of Nations in 1946, South Africa would not comply to relinquish its hold on South West Africa. It took continued pressure from other African states to force the United Nations General Assembly to nullify the mandate. The continued presence of South African administrators and forces led to the formation of a guerrilla movement to make it difficult for South Africa to continue. But it was not until 1988 that South Africa accepted United Nations plans for the independence of what would become Namibia. The United Nations sent in a peacekeeping force to supervise South African withdrawal and the establishment of an electoral process. Independence came on March 21, 1990, shortly before Apartheid in South Africa would be dismantled.

Only the territory of Walvis Bay remained in South African hands for another four years until the new government in a post-Apartheid era relinquished its control.

Namibia has been successful in establishing a government under universal suffrage, and it appears to be working quite well. There are several viable political parties and elections are held on a regular basis at both the federal and local levels. And like South Africa, the government has fostered a policy of reconciliation.

NATIONAL ECONOMY: Mining, limited agriculture and tourism are the cornerstones of the Namibian economy. Despite the stability of the country's political sector, the economy has suffered as a part of the global recession. Unemployment is high, standing at over 30 percent in 2018. Yet despite the high rate of the unemployed, Namibia has been emerging and has been ranked along with countries like Brazil and Mexico as having great potential. Given the limited resource base for agricultural expansion or urban-industrial growth because of aridity, the population density is so low that on a per capita basis, the country looks good with regard to gross domestic product.

Namibia is nearly self-sufficient in food production, as roughly half of the population, primarily rural, depends upon subsistence farming. These are the poor of Namibia who constitute the greater share of the population. To offset this, the smaller, urban population is one of the wealthiest per capita in all of Africa. They rely upon commercial farmers, mainly white, who own nearly half of the arable land of the country, which is a very small percentage in this desert nation. There have been threats of expropriation of much of this agricultural land from the hands of white landowners, but the government recognizes that this could destabilize the country as was true in neighboring Zimbabwe. Another alternative is to begin to tap into unused underground water supplies to provide arable land for many Blacks who would like nothing more than to dispossess white farmers.

The largest sector of the economy is mining. Uranium is the premier mineral that is mined for export, followed by alluvial diamond mining. There are also smaller deposit of copper, zinc, lead, gold, tin and manganese along with limited gas fields that lie offshore.

Tourism is growing each year and has a great potential because of the unique arid and semi-arid landscapes that are essentially undisturbed. Thus ecotourism has a great potential in Namibia. Several ecotourism camps and upmarket lodges have been developing. The country also still allows sport hunting for big game, and there are those who still wish to come to somewhere in Africa for the traditional safari. The cruise industry is only in its infancy with a limited number of ships visiting. It is unfortunate that the more spectacular countryside is located beyond the escarpment and out of reach for ship passengers who only have a single day in port, either in Walvis Bay or Lüderitz.

The next two chapters will describe the two ports of call and detail those activities available to visitors when coming by ship to Namibia.

The dunes of the coastal Namib Desert of Namibia

A giraffe manages to survive on the interior edge of the Namib Desert

The escarpment rib that separates the Namib and Kalahari Deserts

The semi-arid grassland of northeastern Namibia

There is great beauty in the interior mountains near Windhoek

Over the rooftops of Windhoek, (Work of Ji-Elle, CC BY SA 4.0, Wikimedia.org)

A VISIT TO WALVIS BAY

Map of Walvis Bay (© OpenStreetMap contributors)

Walvis Bay is the main port for Namibia, and it has a population of 85,000, but feels like a small Outback Australian town. It is located on the only large natural bay along what is otherwise a relatively strait coast. Behind Walvis Bay and stretching inland to the edge of the Great Escarpment that separates the interior plateau from the sea is a massive sandy desert known as the Namib. This is what geographers call a coastal desert. It forms where cold ocean currents inhibit evaporation and this combines with descending atmospheric high pressure to enhance stability. This is an exceptionally dry desert, and Walvis Bay is one of the driest official urban weather stations on earth. The average rainfall is less than 100 millimeters or four inches per year. And although this is a very dry desert, it is not exceptionally hot right along the coast. Morning fog develops over the sea and drifts onshore, providing droplets of dew that plants have adapted a method of absorption through their leaves rather than their roots. As the day warms, the fog dissipates but temperatures along the coast remain in the 20's to low 30's Celsius or 70's or 80's Fahrenheit. There is very little seasonal variation. This is most unusual for an arid climate, as daily and seasonal changes in temperature are normal desert characteristics. However, inland the desert can become quite hot, especially during the high sun period with temperatures well into the 40's Celsius or 100 degrees plus Fahrenheit .

The offshore waters are rich in nutrients, which attracts a large variety of fish and also Southern right whales. Ultimately this would bring fishermen and whalers to the coastline, and with treacherous currents, many shipwrecked along the dry and desolate coast, known today as the Skeleton Coast. Even today fishing is an important economic activity, and Walvis Bay has a large fishing fleet and processing operations.

LOCAL HISTORY: As noted in the historic sketch for Namibia, the Portuguese were the first to explore along this coastline in the 15th century. But given the nature of what they saw, this was not an area the Crown wished to lay claim to. And the Dutch and later British in South Africa also saw little value in attempting to develop this region. It was not until the major European powers were dividing up Africa into colonial holdings that the Cape Colony claimed the area around Walvis Bay in anticipation of German ambitions since there were few places left for Germany to claim territory.

German colonial ambitions were terminated by the League of Nations at the end of World War I, and the new Union of South Africa was given a mandate over South West Africa. Prior to the start of the war, the Cape Colony and Germany became embroiled in a struggle over the boundaries of the Walvis Bay territory. During the war, German forces did invade Walvis Bay, but the South Africans reclaimed it in 1915, thus giving the League of Nations the impetus for naming the Union as the guardian of the former German territory. However, South Africa attempted to claim that it was a part of their nation.

The United Nations had cancelled South Africa's mandate after World War II, but to forestall losing Walvis Bay, the Parliament transferred control of it directly to the Cape Province as an exclave - a detached piece of its territory.

In 1977, the South African government reasserted its direct control over the Walvis Bay area, claiming sovereign right by its original annexation during the late 19th century. But the United Nations imposed a mandate for the government to negotiate with the newly forming Namibia for return of Walvis Bay, which was finally accomplished in 1994 just following the end of the Apartheid Era.

Today Walvis Bay is the second city of Namibia and its only major port, connected to the interior capital city of Windhoek by a narrow gauge railroad. Both imports and exports are channeled by rail between the interior and the port. And there is overnight passenger service between Walvis Bay and Windhoek, the only passenger rail service in the country.

WHAT TO DO AND SEE: Frankly there is absolutely nothing for visitors to see in Walvis Bay that would take more than an hour. The main activity for cruise passengers is to take one of the ship's tours out into the unique and mysterious sandy Namib Desert, or to visit the old German town of Swakopmund, which has become a tourist destination. Walvis Bay is an industrial port, and the city has a small downtown, mostly composed of more modern one-story buildings. It resembles a typical Outback town that you would see in Australia. This is a working class city, as the port, fishing fleet and processing plants provide the majority of employment. Most cruise lines do offer a shuttle into the heart of Walvis Bay since it is not possible to walk through the busy port.

* For those who want to have a private car and driver/guide, it is doubtful that the ship's tour office will have any arrangement capabilities. I recommend that you check on line with Turnstone Tours at www.turnstone-tours.com for information regarding their privately arranged day tours. They are located in Swakopmund, but it is only a short 30 minute drive for them to come pick up guests at the ship. Another company that will arrange private party tours is Mola Namibia. Their web page is www.mola-namibia.com where you can see their offerings.

* You can rent a self-driving car in Walvis Bay and get around to the major sights on your own. Road traffic is minimal and the distances are not great. Road signs are all written in English. But keep in mind that Namibian traffic also flows on the left just as in South Africa and if you have never driven on the left, it can be difficult on the open road where you would pass slower moving cars on the right. I do not recommend it for first time drivers on the left.

* There are no taxi companies in Walvis Bay. The closest approximation are shuttle services that provide airport transfers. One company called Execu-Cab Tours & Transfers may be capable of providing local touring. Check their web page at www.execu-cab.com.

* If you only wish to stay in town, which frankly is a waste of a day, you can easily walk the whole of central Walvis Bay once you take the ship shuttle into the center.

All of the ship tours involve leaving Walvis Bay, as the major sights are within an hour of the city, but out in the desert. My recommendations for those who will be hiring a car and driver/guide are as follows (shown alphabetically):

* Living Desert Tour in a 4x4 - There are often tours out beyond the dunes toward the Great Escarpment where you have a chance to see some of the unique plant and animal life of the interior of the Namib Desert. These are either half or full day tours offered through your cruise line.

* Mondesa Township - This cultural tour, if your ship offers it, would give you a chance to visit what was a former Black only township. It is still a depressed community, but is trying to entice visitors to see how people live and to encourage a better understanding of the economic differences that still often follow racial lines.

* Pelican Point - This point is at the end of a long sand spit. The waters abound in seals, dolphins and of course pelicans. The best way to enjoy the wildlife is to kayak in the calm

waters. But once again, most ship tours will only offer sightseeing as part of a wider half or full-day exploration. Some cruise lines do offer more adventurous tours to Pelican Point.

* Sand Dune Number Seven - The world's tallest sand dune, located in a field of major dunes, is one of the top attractions outside of Walvis Bay. This is a great area for sand boarding and quad bikes, but generally most ship tours offer just a short glimpse of the dunes with no time for adventure, but to have that amount of time you would need to first have arranged for a car and driver/guide.

* Namib- Naukluft National Park, a vast sea of tall dunes that provide for spectacular photography. The park begins south of Walvis Bay and covers as vast area of coastal sand dunes and stretches toward the interior. Again you can only visit with ease if your ship has a tour arranged or if you have booked a private car and driver/guide or small group tour.

* Skeleton Coast - If your cruise line offers an all day tour north to the Skeleton Coast, this would be an amazing adventure. This wild coastline is both beautiful and forbidding. Visiting would put you among a mere handful of tourists who have ever seen this starkly beautiful landscape because it begins north of Swakopmund and a visit becomes a long day tour.

* Sossusvlei Dunes - Again this is another field of immense sand dunes, large crescent shapes that rise as high as 330 meters or 1,000 feet, making them the largest collection of such dunes in the world. The tours are generally made in 4x4 vehicles due to the nature of the terrain, but to reach the park first requires a short flight southeast from Walvis Bay to Sesriem, which not all cruise lines will offer. The star attraction is Dune 45, which visitors are allowed to climb.

* Swakopmund - The third city of Namibia is less than an hour away from Walvis Bay. This was a major German colonial outpost since the South Africans had control over Walvis Bay. As the major colonial town on the coast, it exhibits beautiful examples of traditional German architecture from the late 19th century, but adapted to the desert environment. It has developed into a popular beachfront community and has many quaint cafes, gift shops, guesthouses, hotels and museums and definitely is oriented to selling its architecture and Germanic flavor. This is the last place you would expect to find Bavarian chocolates, or good German beer. Swakopmund also has beautiful beaches, and if you are looking for a quiet day this would be my recommendation, but you will need a car and driver/guide. Many of the dune tours do spend an hour or so in Swakopmund, but that does not give you time to really enjoy the community.

I strongly urge you to consider a tour while in Walvis Bay. If you just stay in the main town area, you will quickly run out of sights to see.

DINING OUT: If you are staying in Walvis Bay or returning after a half-day tour, you may wish to enjoy lunch in town. Surprisingly there are a handful of relatively nice restaurants, primarily featuring seafood, from which to choose. I have listed my few favorites followed by a few listings for Swakopmund, as some tours allow time for lunch. And some of you may have a car and driver/guide taking you north along the sand dune coast. Swakopmund is an ideal spot for lunch. In both sets of listings, the arrangement is alphabetical as usual.

WALVIS BAY:

* Anchors @ the Jetty – This seafood restaurant is located on Esplanade Street right at the edge of the edge of the Walvis Bay Waterfront. It offers consistently good seafood served in a friendly atmosphere and at reasonable prices. The restaurant also has vegan and vegetarian offerings as well as the freshest of local seafood. And for you meat lovers, you will also find a few meaty offerings. The restaurant is open Tuesday thru Saturday from 11 AM to 10 PM and Sunday from 11 AM to 9 PM.

* Flamingo Bay Restaurant – Located a bit farther along the shore south of the Lagoon at 30 Kavambo Nujoma Drive in the Meersig Extension, this is a very excellent European and Continental restaurant that is also vegetarian friendly. It is part of the Villa Flamingo Hotel but diners are always welcome. The level of the cuisine and its presentation will surprise most visitors, as they do not expect this level of sophistication in Walvis Bay. They serve from 7 AM to 10 PM daily, including breakfast since this is a hotel restaurant.

* Raft – Clearly another fine seafood restaurant on the Esplanade at the Lagoon, the Raft is also well respected by locals for its fresh seafood. You will be dining over the water and will like the casual atmosphere. They are open Monday thru Saturday from 11 AM to 11 PM and on Sunday from 11 AM to 2 PM for lunch only.

* Willie Probst Bakery, Café & Restaurant – Located in the downtown core of Walvis Bay at 1C Theo Ben Gurirab Street this combination German bakery and café serves a diverse menu of sandwiches, burgers and a wide array of cakes and pastries. This is a good place to stop in for a light lunch or afternoon tea when in the city center. They are open Monday thru Friday from 6:30 AM to 5:45 PM and Saturday from 6:30 AM to 2 PM.

SWAKOPMUND:

* Hansa Hotel – This beautiful Old World hotel is located in the heart of town at 3 Hendrik Witbooi Street. Their dining room serves spectacular lunches from an exhaustive menu that is still written in German and English. They offer starters, salads, soups, a variety of mains including meats, poultry and seafood and desserts. It is recommended to have the ship's concierge or your driver, if in a private car, book ahead for lunch. They do not post their hours, but lunch is generally served around Noon and continues until 2 PM.

* Ocean Cellar – Facing out over the bay in the Strand Hotel, this beautiful dining room is open to the freshness of the sea. Their menu features a wide array of fresh seafood prepared to perfection. They also offer vegetarian dishes. Sushi and oysters are specialties and their hot entrees are very diverse with one chicken and one beef entrée, otherwise seafood rules. They serve daily from Noon to 10 PM.

* **Old Steamer Restaurant** – Located in the Alte Bruke Resort on Strand Street South, which is just a short walk from the heart of the commercial area where most tour busses stop, this is a very well respected restaurant known for its outstanding cuisine. The menu is quite diverse and their buffet will surprise you as a visitor for its lavish quality. You will be tempted to overindulge, but after all you are on holiday. They are only open in the evening Monday thru Saturday from 6 to 10 PM, but some cruise ships do stay in Walvis Bay into the evening, or depending upon the itinerary even overnight. If you have a dinner option and have transportation, this is a worthwhile choice.

* **Village Café** – In the heart of town at 21 Sam Nujoma Avenue, this international style café serves outstanding cuisine, some say the best in town. It is very popular for its diverse menu and freshness, and it also offers vegetarian friendly dishes. It is open Monday thru Thursday from 7 AM to 5 PM, Friday from 6 AM to 5 PM and Saturday from 7 AM to 1:30 PM.

FINAL WORDS: I have been to Walvis Bay numerous times. The actual town is rather pleasant, but offers no special sights. The waterfront is pleasant along the bay and does offer fine dining options. But I highly recommend that you take a tour out into the Namib Desert, as this is the main reason for the port being on your itinerary. The Namib is unlike all other deserts in the world because of its utter starkness and its massive coastal dunes.

Other than having a fine meal, staying in town for the whole day will be a day wasted. If you do not want to go on a desert tour, at least visit Swakopmund either on a ship supported tour or with a car and driver/guide for half a day. Swakopmund does exude much of the charm of its former German colonial heritage.

THE COMMERCIAL HEART OF WALVIS BAY

The downtown core of Walvis Bay

This map is best viewed directly from OpenStreetMap.com on your personal device where it can be expanded or one specific area can be enlarged. Given the format of this book, it is impossible to display maps with the level of detail you might wish to have while actually out exploring the city. But the OpenStreetMap maps used directly are the tool I always rely upon.

THE CITY OF SWAKOMOND

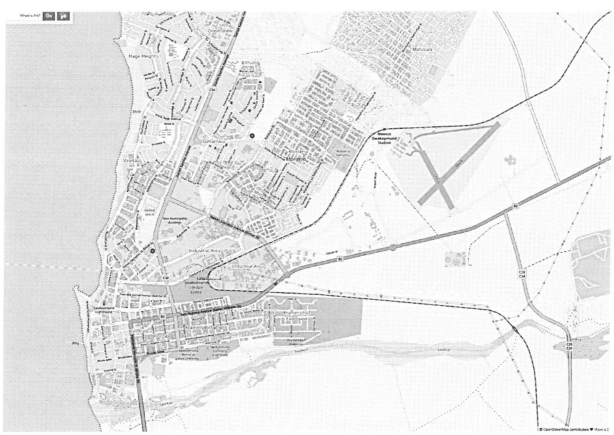

The city of Swakopmund

This map is best viewed directly from OpenStreetMap.com on your personal device where it can be expanded or one specific area can be enlarged. Given the format of this book, it is impossible to display maps with the level of detail you might wish to have while actually out exploring the city. But the OpenStreetMap maps used directly are the tool I always rely upon.

THE COMMERCIAL HEART OF SWAKOPMUND

The downtown core of Swakopmund

This map is best viewed directly from OpenStreetMap.com on your personal device where it can be expanded or one specific area can be enlarged. Given the format of this book, it is impossible to display maps with the level of detail you might wish to have while actually out exploring the city. But the OpenStreetMap maps used directly are the tool I always rely upon.

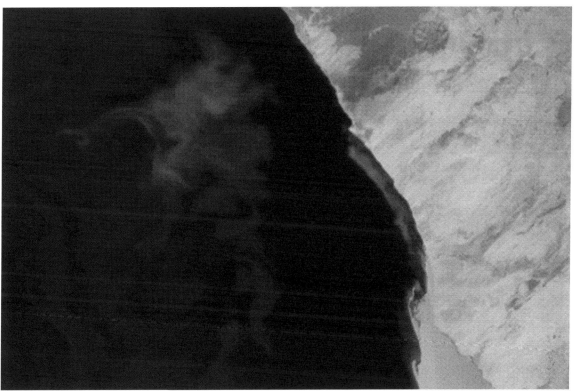
Satellite view of the stark coast of Namibia at Swakopmund

The busy port of Walvis Bay, Namibia's window to the world

In the heart of downtown Walvis Bay

The grounds of the Walvis Bay Town Hall

Walvis Bay surrounded by dunes, (Work of Laika ac, CC BY SA 2.0, Wikimedia.org)

A freight train leaves Walvis Bay bound across the desert for Windhoek

A typical street in Swakopmund

Swakopmund's German architecture, (Work of Olga Emst, CCBY SA 4.0, Wikimedia.org)

The coastal dunes between Walvis Bay and Swakopmund (Work of Hansueli Krapf, CC BY SA 3.0, Wikimedia.org)

STOPPING IN REMOTE LÜDERITZ

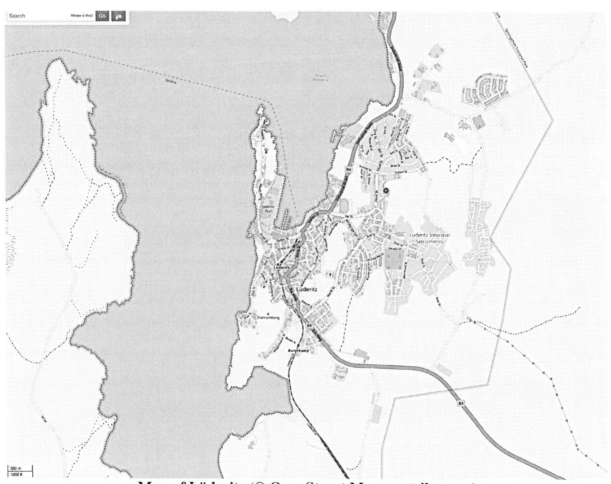

Map of Lüderitz (© OpenStreet Map contributors)

The only other port on the Namibian coast capable of docking a cruise ship is Lüderitz. This very Germanic settlement is situated in the southern Namib Desert, in an area that is somewhat rocky, having several outcrops and small offshore islands that provide for a small anchorage rather than the broad port at Walvis Bay. The small harbor is quite shallow and has a rocky bottom, thus only smaller ships such as those of the upmarket cruise lines are capable of sailing into the dock.

Lüderitz is a small city with only 12,600 residents. And it is especially isolated from both Walvis Bay and Windhoek, though it does have a road connection to the inland capital, but the journey is long and very empty. This is the smallest port you will visit, that is if your cruise ship will even stop here, as most do not.

The question you may be thinking of at the moment is why come here. And that would be quite valid. But Lüderitz is making quite an attempt to lure smaller cruise ships to dock so that their passengers can experience a taste of German architecture in a rather picturesque setting that is very different from the flat landscape of Swakopmund or Walvis Bay. And just inland is the former diamond-mining town of Kolmanskop that is today a true ghost town being swallowed by the sands of the Namib Desert. But for the sake of appealing to visitors, the local tourist board does battle with the sand to maintain the site, which is quite fascinating and a bit romantic like the ghost towns of the American West.

Like Walvis Bay, the climate of Lüderitz is truly arid, but with the maritime fog in the morning bringing limited moisture to local plant life, and helping keep the temperatures moderate. But just inland by at most 20 kilometers the summers can be exceptionally parched and hot.

LOCAL HISTORY: Although early Portuguese and Dutch explorers scouted along the coast, and Bartolomeu Dias even planted a small cross in 1487, the area was seen as too forbidding for settlement. The Dutch did, however, recognize the immense fishing and whaling potential off the coast, but still never established a town in the area of what would become Lüderitz. It was not until 1883 when the site was purchased in the name of Adolf Lüderitz. One of his operatives made the purchase from the local Nama tribal chief. But Adolf Lüderitz never returned from an expedition he undertook inland in 1886 and in his honor the town was then named.

The actual development of the town represents a very dark side to German colonial history. Between 1905 and 1907, they established a prison camp on Shark Island off the coast of Lüderitz, using the town as the port from the shipment of native Herero and Nama people to the island to be literally worked to death. Essentially the prison was a death camp, a means of obtaining labor while insuring the elimination of the native people. It is ironic that it would foreshadow what would come back in Germany during World War II.

In 1909, diamonds were discovered inland at Kolmanskop, and this brought Lüderitz into importance as the port for entry to the diamond fields. In 1915 when South Africa took over the mandate for South West Africa, the German population was deported. Diamonds continued to be discovered in the interior, but never became economically significant as to insure that Lüderitz would develop into a major community.

SEEING THE SIGHTS: There is little for the visitor to do or see in Lüderitz, but an hour or two of exploration does produce some wonderful pictures of traditional German architecture set against an arid landscape, and in the afternoon the sky becomes quite blue and cloudless. Most cruise lines that stop in Lüderitz generally offer a tour out to the ghost town of Kolmanskop, a journey that gives you a chance to see some of the starkly dramatic countryside and also explore the remains of this once thriving German diamond mining camp that is today being swallowed by shifting sand dunes. I highly recommend the tour, as it only takes half of the day, leaving the rest of the day to simply wander around Lüderitz and enjoy its distinctive architectural flavor.

* The town of Lüderitz is so small that you do not need a car and driver/guide to get around. Even if you have somewhat limited mobility, you can enjoy the central part of the town with its distinctive architectural flavor. I highly doubt that you could obtain a car and driver/guide, as they would have to come from Windhoek, which is a long distance away.*

* There is a taxi service in Lüderitz that generally transfers passengers between town and the airport, but you may be able to prearrange a sightseeing tour. The company is called IHate Taxi and their web page is *www.IHatetaxi.com* and they have a contact icon. They may even be able to offer a private tour to Kolmanskop.

The recommended sights in Lüderitz apart from a visit out to Kolmanskop are as follows (shown alphabetically):

* Deutsche Afrika Bank – This incredible building is a classic example of grand bank architecture in the early 20th century, built in 1907.

* Felsenkirche - The beautiful and rather grand but small Lutheran church on a hill overlooking Lüderitz with striking views of the surroundings. The interior can only be viewed Monday thru Saturday from 5 to 6 PM unless it happens to be open earlier on the day you visit.

* Goerke House – This is a prominent 19th century German mansion sitting on a hill overlooking the town. It offers a glimpse into what it must have been like to live as a wealthy person in an otherwise mundane town. Hans Goerke was co-owner of one of the diamond mines. Check locally as to hours of operation before walking up the hill, as its opening and closing times are a bit erratic. Their official times are Monday thru Friday 2 to 4 PM and Saturday and Sunday from 4 to 6 PM.

* Lüderitz Museum - This is a very small and somewhat forgotten museum that sees few visitors apart from when a ship is in port. It does provide you with a look into the short lived glory of Lüderitz, The museum is open weekdays from 3:30 to 5 PM.

* Lüderitz Railway Station - Today this important building is a national monument. Once the rail line connected Lüderitz with Windhoek, but today parts of the line have fallen into disrepair. The government has planned to repair the line, as it would aid in tourists coming to Lüderitz from the capital of Windhoek. No posted hours are shown for the building.

You may think that the minimal number of attractions in Lüderitz will make this a wasted stop. But I promise that you will find this small former German settlement quite worthwhile.

DINING OUT: There are only a few restaurants in Lüderitz and I have chosen the three best where you can have a nice lunch while visiting the town. My choices, in alphabetical order, are:

* Diaz Coffee Shop – AT 25 Bismarck Street in the heart of town, this nice café serves international style cuisine including German schnitzel and sausage, outstanding desserts and a variety of coffees. For American tastes, they do make a fairly good hamburger. Their menu is vegetarian friendly. They are open daily from 8 AM to 8 PM.

* Garden Café – At 17 Hafen Street near the harbor, this European type café offers nice salads, quiche, baked chicken and other delectable light food items for lunch along with very good traditional German style desserts. They are open from 7 AM to 5PM weekdays, 7 AM to 4 PM on Saturday and from 9 AM to 3 PM on Sunday.

* Oyster and Wine Bar – In town at 25 Bismarck Street, associated with Diaz Coffee Shop, this restaurant features fresh local seafood, and as its name implies, oysters are a specialty. It is open daily from 8 AM to 8 PM.

FINAL WORDS: Lüderitz is a quaint and very distinctive small German colonial town with very distinctive architecture. It is trying to make a comeback as a tourist oriented community, but it does not really have much to offer at the moment other than its unique architecture.

A visit to the now totally deserted town of Kolmanskop gives you the experience of visiting an African ghost town being swallowed by the desert. I must say it is a unique experience.

THE CITY OF LÜDERITZ

The city of Lüderitz

This map is best viewed directly from OpenStreetMap.com on your personal device where it can be expanded or one specific area can be enlarged. Given the format of this book, it is impossible to display maps with the level of detail you might wish to have while actually out exploring the city. But the OpenStreetMap maps used directly are the tool I always rely upon.

Sailing into Lüderitz

The fishing fleet at anchor in Lüderitz

The Bismarck Strasse in the heart of Lüderitz

A close up of the old railway station on Bismarck Strasse

A view over Lüderitz from the Felsenkirch

The beautiful old Felsenkirch

One of the many old German colonial mansions

The remains of Kolmanskop (Work of Joachim Huber, CC BY SA 2.0, Wikimedia.org)

The now deserted Kolmanskop, (Work of Zairon, CC BY SA 4.0, Wikimedia.org)

Kolmanskop is a true ghost town (Work of Sara&Joachim, CC BY SA 2.0, Wikimedia.org)

FINAL WORDS

For both North Americans and Europeans, it is a long way from home to South Africa. But a visit is nothing less than a memorable experience. The natural landscape is breathtaking, giving the country a sense of drama and sheer beauty that is hard to match in many other parts of the world. The people are very welcoming, gracious and friendly. Yes there is the worry about becoming a victim of petty crime, but most tourists never experience anything bad because of taking simple precautions.

The best way to lessen the magnitude of the journey is to take an extended cruise from one of Europe's Mediterranean ports down either the west or east coast of Africa culminating in a visit to all of the ports herein discussed. Such a cruise takes at least five weeks, and it is not possible for most people to be away from home for that length of time. In that event, it is necessary to fly both ways between home and South Africa, and this factor often dissuades people from planning a South African adventure. All I can say, is do not let the long flights be the factor that turns you away from a visit to this beautiful country.

ABOUT THE AUTHOR

Dr. Lew Deitch

I am a semi-retired professor of geography with over 46 years of teaching experience. During my distinguished career, I directed the Honors Program at Northern Arizona University and developed many programs relating to the study of contemporary world affairs. I am an honors graduate of The University of California, Los Angeles, earned my Master of Arts at The University of Arizona and completed my doctorate in geography at The University of New England in Australia. I am a globetrotter, having visited 97countries on all continents except Antarctica. My primary focus is upon human landscapes, especially such topics as local architecture, foods, clothing and folk music. I am also a student of world politics and conflict.

I enjoy being in front of an audience, and have spoken to thousands of people at civic and professional organizations. I have been lecturing on board ships for a major five star cruise line since 2008. I love to introduce people to exciting new places both by means of presenting vividly illustrated talks and through serving as a tour consultant for ports of call. I am also an avid writer, and for years I have written my own text books used in my university classes. Now I have turned my attention to writing travel companions, books that will introduce you to the country you are visiting, but not serving as a touring book like the major guides you find in all of the bookstores.

I also love languages, and my skills include a conversational knowledge of German, Russian and Spanish.

I am a dual Canadian-American with two passports, and I was raised in California, have lived in Canada and Australia. Arizona has been his permanent home since 1974. One exciting aspect of my life was the ten-year period, during which I volunteered my time as an Arizona Highway Patrol reserve trooper, working out on the streets and highways and also developing new safety and enforcement programs for use statewide. I presently live just outside of Phoenix in the beautiful resort city of Scottsdale.

TO CONTACT ME, PLEASE CHECK OUT MY WEB PAGE FOR MORE INFORMATION AT:
http://www.doctorlew.com

Made in the USA
Columbia, SC
15 November 2021